TOUCHING ON
CHRISTIAN TRUTH

TOUCHING ON CHRISTIAN TRUTH

THE KINGDOM OF GOD, THE CHRISTIAN CHURCH
AND THE WORLD

by

Archbishop Lord Fisher of Lambeth

A. R. MOWBRAY & CO LIMITED
LONDON AND OXFORD

© *A. R. Mowbray & Co Ltd 1971*
Printed in Great Britain at the Pitman Press, Bath
First published in 1971
SBN 264 64537 5

241 3/6
F 53

Contents

PART ONE:
THE KINGDOM OF GOD

I

Wayfaring

SAUL, later called Paul, first comes into the history of the Christian Church when he is mentioned as witnessing the stoning to death of Stephen and approving of it. Next we are told that still breathing threats and murder against the disciples of the Lord, Saul went to the High Priest in Jerusalem and asked him for letters to the synagogues at Damascus, so that 'if he found any belonging to the Way, men or women, he might bring them bound to Jerusalem'. Saul after his conversion to the Christian faith[1] was called by Barnabas to help him in looking after the Church in Antioch where the disciples were for the first time called Christians; but an earlier description of them was that they were followers of the Way. Perhaps this was due to memories of the teaching of Jesus Christ who spoke of himself as the Way, the Truth and the Life and told his disciples that 'the gate is narrow and the way is hard that leads to life, and those who find it are few'.

In a very oecumenical prayer contained in the Book of Common Prayer, we pray for the good estate of the Catholic Church; 'that it may be so guided and governed by thy good spirit, that all who profess and call themselves Christians may be led into the way of truth, and hold the faith in unity of spirit, in the bond of peace, and in righteousness of life'.

---

[1] For the record of St. Paul's own accounts of his conversion, see Acts of the Apostles, chapters 9 and 26.

Here are great words, which take us to the very heart of the Christian faith and of the Will of God—unity, peace, righteousness of life, but at their head is the Way of Truth: and by Truth is meant not a series of definitions or ideas but the Spirit of Truth.

We are told that Jesus Christ had a brief conversation with Pontius Pilate before he was finally sentenced to death. Christ's last word was 'Everyone who is of the truth hears my voice': and the last word of all was Pilate's 'What is truth?'

There are many kinds of truth, all of them hard to come by. It is commonly supposed that the hardest and most elusive of all is the truth about God. The Christian Church knows what Jesus Christ taught about God, and there are the great main roads of Christian doctrine running through the history of the Church: but they run across great tracts of moorland and mountain. Those who are in a hurry or like to travel with their luggage at hand will be wise to stick to the main roads and the macadam. But most of us, in fact, like to make our own way across country, with a map in our pockets to tell us where the main roads are and by which we can check our general direction. We do not want to know our exact position at any time, but we do want to feel satisfied that we are not lost. None of us can answer that question 'What is truth?' But a Christian, called by his own instinct and initiative to get away from the beaten track, to walk in the freedom of the Christian spirit, to go across country, wants to be certain all the same that he is in the Way, the way of Christian truth—walking in the right direction. Every Christian minister has his own personal knowledge of the country of our pilgrimage and has his own chosen tracks and short cuts which he uses for himself. In what follows

I set down some of the results of my wayfaring. I quote no authorities and claim no authority: but these are where my feet have taken me on my pilgrimage and I claim only that by the grace of God I have not departed from the right general direction, or from the Way of truth.[1]

2

The Kingdom

HOWEVER long and complicated a journey may be, one has to start from somewhere. So much is said about religion in general and the Christian religion in particular, from so many different points of view and leading to so many different conclusions or non-conclusions, that one may feel and many do feel that it is impossible to know where to start in about the Christian faith. I have found my own starting-point. It is in the New Testament of course: for the only record that we have of Christ and of the origins of Christianity is in the books of the New Testament. One of the greatest preachers of the Christian faith in its formative days was St. Paul. The last we hear of him was when he was in Rome under house arrest, having appealed to Caesar for justice (being by birth a

---

[1] In a letter recently received from a bishop, I read 'a young person has said to me, "Of course now the issue is not reunion, but God. I have lost my earlier enthusiasm for the former because of my concern for the latter." I very much agreed.' That was very immature of the bishop. Enthusiasm must always be (by definition of the word) from and for God. But the mature Christian must realise that responsible leaders show their enthusiasm for God by the meticulous care and foresight and hindsight with which they feed the flock of Christ. They must be expert caterers as well as shepherds.

Roman citizen as well as a Jew) against the accusation of the Jewish authorities in Jerusalem. The final words of the book called The Acts of the Apostles are these:

> And he (Paul) lived there (in Rome) two whole years at his own expense and welcomed all who came to him, preaching the kingdom of God and teaching about the Lord Jesus Christ quite openly and unhindered.

St. Paul preached about the kingdom of God, because that had been what Jesus Christ had preached about. It was the one thing that Jesus proclaimed. There, eternal, invisible, spiritual, real, was, is and ever shall be the kingdom of God. There for the Christian, everything begins and ends. And one can safely say that no one here on earth can possibly prove that it does not exist or that its existence is improbable![1]

What Christ said about that kingdom can be discovered from the four gospels contained in the New Testament—or (to be completely accurate) from what the writers of these gospels were able to put on record of the teaching of Christ as it was remembered and handed on by his first disciples. There can be no doubt whatsoever that the main theme of all he did and said was this kingdom of God. I need only quote the one saying: 'seek first God's kingdom and his righteousness, and all these (other) things shall be yours as well'. Christ included, in his model prayer, the words 'Thy kingdom come'.

Beyond all doubt Jesus Christ claimed to know about this kingdom from the inside and to have authority in it. His first disciples recognised and accepted that claim with utter conviction, and expressed it when they came to speak

---

[1] Bertrand Russell, a very great philosopher, denied that there was this kingdom of God. He did not disprove it. What he did prove was that while a fervent humanitarian, he was ignorant in much that belongs to the kingdom of God.

of Jesus as Lord and as Son of God. Of course being Jews by birth and upbringing, they also spoke of him as Messiah, fulfiller of all the hopes and promises recorded in the Old Testament: but to non-Jews (the Gentiles) he was known from the start as Our Lord Jesus Christ, who had opened the way for all who believed in him, into the kingdom to which, after his crucifixion and resurrection, he had returned to glory.

So Christian faith affirms that the man Jesus Christ came from that kingdom of God on high (in the heavens) beyond all time and space, and has returned to it, there to dwell 'at the right hand of the Majesty on high'. That is all that human language can do to describe the coming and going of this revealer and of this kingdom of God. Certainly no man has done more, or done as much, to reveal and testify to the existence and the nature of that kingdom. But of course the significance of this kingdom rests on the fact that it belongs to God. Who then, is God?

3

God the Father

ONCE, arriving at an airport in Australia, I was shown by reporters a newspaper cutting in which an Australian Professor of Science was recorded as saying in a lecture that God *was* the universe. The reporters asked me to comment; and being at the end of a long journey I did so in the fewest possible words, saying that the Professor was talking nonsense. Later I corresponded with the Professor and found he was a Christian and a worshipper of the God and Father of our Lord Jesus Christ. What he meant was that he found the handiwork of God present in the processes of the natural universe; wonderful beyond words in their majesty and beauty, and that he worshipped God who had created such a wonderful universe: but what he *said* was nonsense. If there is a God who is in any reasonable contact with us, he must be not only a power of the universe but the power beyond the universe, outside and above it. From long before the time of Christ up to this present time the philosophers have speculated as to whether there is a God and if so how to conceive of his nature and his activities: and such speculation will continue to the end of man's history. On a more recent visit to Australia, a reporter recalling the earlier episode, asked me what I had to say about atheism. I replied that 'I had nothing to say about nothing'; for atheism is a purely negative statement that God does not exist—and you cannot really talk about non-existence in terms of human relations.

And here is the point of importance. Jesus Christ talked of God only in terms of his relation to us human beings, that is to say in personal terms; and he talked of the kingdom of God only in terms relevant to personal behaviour, whether God's behaviour or ours. It is very right that philosophers and theologians should speculate about the being and powers of God, the ultimate Being, and about the nature of existence and of knowledge. It is a very healthy exercise, but exercise can be overdone. It is very right that theologians should in particular speculate about the general relation of God to Man and especially to problems of human suffering, sin and survival. And of course from youth upwards we are all in some measure theologians and are all trying to some extent to be philosophers. It is very right that St. Paul, as a philosopher and theologian, should speak of Jesus Christ as 'the image of the invisible God, the first born of all creation' who is 'before all things and in him all things hold together', and that St. Paul should say that in Christ 'all the fullness of God was pleased to dwell'. But it must be recognised that this is Christian philosophy or metaphysics; and that all philosophic and metaphysical speculation is engaged in the seeking of answers to questions which can never be finally answered in terms of human understanding, and which can only be formulated in human terms. If by 'the fullness of God' is meant a full understanding of all that could be known about God, and his operations, then we can certainly not find it in Jesus Christ; and it is misleading to suggest that it can be or ought to be found there. It is not to be found in Jesus Christ because he did not mean that it should be found in him, nor could it be expressed by him in the terms of his ministry on earth. St. Paul says also that though Jesus Christ was in essence God, he did

not cling to his essential Godhead but for the purpose of
his mission to this world 'emptied himself, taking the form
of a servant, being born in the likeness of men'. That is
metaphysics again: but for our purposes, it is enough to
say that Jesus Christ brought himself within our compre-
hension. He limited himself to revealing or declaring only
one aspect of God Almighty or God All-power or God All-
being, and that aspect was the one which alone is of
essential importance to we men in our daily lives—and
there it is in the opening words of the prayer which he
gave us: 'Our Father (who art) in Heaven'. It is recorded
by St. John that on the first Easter Day Jesus Christ
appeared to Mary Magdalene in the garden of the resurrection and said 'go to my brethren and say to them, I am
ascending to my Father and your Father, to my God and
your God'. Again leaving the metaphysics aside, this
means that Jesus Christ put himself on a level with us in
calling God our Father, ours as well as his. Quite clearly,
since he spoke so confidently of the kingdom of God, the
idea of the Fatherhood of God conveyed far more to him
than it can to us—but for us it is all in its nature Fatherhood: and he could say, without creating any kind of misunderstanding, that 'He who has seen me has seen the
Father', and 'Believe me that I am in the Father and the
Father in me; or else believe me for the sake of the works
themselves'; and 'The words that I say to you I do not
speak on my own authority: but the Father who dwells
in me does his works (through me)'.

Now it does not matter whether Jesus Christ ever spoke
precisely these words to Mary in the garden, or to his
disciples in answer to a question put to him by Philip, as
St. John records. There is no doubt that St. John is here
expressing the reality of the impression which the disciples

gained from living with Jesus Christ and hearing him talk
and preach. By the words *Father* (applied to God Almighty) and *Son of God* (applied to himself) Jesus Christ
meant us to understand not only that he and his Father
were one in the Godhead but that his Father was our
Father also and made known to us as such 'through Jesus
Christ our Lord'. So St. Peter expresses one aspect of the
coinage of the Christian faith when he writes 'Blessed be
the God and Father of our Lord Jesus Christ who by his
great mercy has begotten us again to a living hope through
the resurrection of Jesus Christ from the dead, to an inheritance which is imperishable, undefiled, and unfading
kept in heaven for you.' And our Lord himself reveals
another aspect of the same coinage when he teaches us to
pray to 'Our Father, who art in heaven . . . Give us this
day our daily bread.'

Of that Fatherhood, one thing is above all evident—
that it creates a personal link between God our Father and
his Son Jesus Christ on the one hand, and with every single
person, born of a woman into the human family, on the
other. It must never be forgotten that this link with God
through the Holy Spirit, the Lord, the Giver of Life, is the
birthright of every human being of every class, colour or
creed granted by God himself.[1] That is why a prayer in the
Church of England Communion service begins so rightly
'Almighty and everliving God who . . . has taught us to
make prayers and supplications, and to give thanks, for
all men.'

I shall not attempt here to expound all that is meant to
us by the fact that God is thus the Father of all of us

---

[1] Man is not born into the world with any inherent rights—only duties.
Whatever 'rights' he comes to acquire he acquires either from God or from
his fellow men or from some group of his fellow men.

separately and collectively, I shall try only to indicate in the next two chapters how two essential needs of all of us in our human condition are met by the assurance which Jesus Christ gives to us that there is a kingdom of God, eternal in the heavens, that God, who there reigns, is before all else Our Father, and that the way into that kingdom is open to us all.

No one can prove that there is any kind of life after a man dies. It may be final extinction. I am sure that it is not. Of course I believe that every man born of a woman when he dies goes to the eternal kingdom of God. There is nowhere else for him to go. What happens to each of us when we get there is another story: but I am quite sure that we are received into the kingdom not by a posse of policemen of the spiritual world but by a friendly group of social workers of the spiritual world or of its doctors and nurses or the like, for we shall all be a bit bruised and some terribly torn and broken when we arrive. The Church must confess honestly that it has done immense harm all through the ages by its teaching about hell and punishment and by misguided teaching about guilt. It was done with the best of motives. Now, thank God, we all know better than to teach or to believe it. Because God is love, all treatment there will be in essence remedial.

4

Personal Fulfilment

THERE is much debate nowadays as to whether there is a future life for us men on the other side of death: and the more it is debated, the more doubtful the prospect seems to become. Of course, the scientific evidence for any worthwhile kind of life beyond death hardly exists. There is some evidence that points to some kind of a personal survival, but that leaves it still as no more than a matter of surmise—a wishful thinking: and in any case if the future life is a reality, it is impossible for us to put into words any definite picture of what it means to live it. It must be said that some of the ecclesiastical descriptions of the world beyond carry little conviction—even where they do not repel. So it is that the clergy now speak little of the future life and many practising Christians seem to have no real belief in it.

In the Creed we profess our belief that 'on the third day' Christ rose from the dead and we go on to say 'and I look for the Resurrection of the dead, and the Life of the world to come'. I believe in the truth of the accounts of Christ's resurrection given in the gospels; I believe in the empty tomb; I believe that Christ rose from the dead taking his physical body with him. Why not? I accept St. Paul's testimony to the fact of his resurrection. It happened as an objective fact. Christ, risen from the dead, showed himself in person to his disciples and spoke with them. When St. Peter invited the small company of Christians after Christ's ascension to elect someone to take the place left vacant by

the death of Judas Iscariot among the Apostles, he said
that the one chosen 'must become with us a witness to his
resurrection'. Christians very rightly have always based
their belief in the future life on the resurrection of Christ.
As the hymn says, 'Christ is risen, we are risen'. But it is
still an act of faith. It is possible to say that the evidence
for Christ's resurrection is insufficient, that it rests on
hearsay, that it may be no more than the projection as a
physical fact of a spiritual experience, and so forth. All
this is said again and again in the continuing debate and
has power if not to overthrow the Christian's faith in a
future life, at least to rob it of its conviction. He finds himself with no effective weapons with which to defend a
positive belief in a future life, even while he clings to it as
an act of faith.

There is another consideration. Even though the resurrection of Christ is accepted, as I accept it, as a real
physical fact of immense spiritual significance, it cannot be
regarded as directly applicable to us. The physical body of
Christ was, according to the record, taken up and transmuted into a spiritual possession of Christ, no longer norm-
ally visible. Our physical bodies after death are physical
still and subject to corruption. This obvious fact has led to
great perplexities and confusion in Christian thought
through the ages. 'The resurrection of the dead' in one
creed becomes 'the resurrection of the body' in another,
and 'all men must rise again with their bodies' in another.
St. Paul, in the famous chapter 15 of I Corinthians, says
of the physical body that after death 'it is sown in dis-
honour, it is raised in glory, it is sown a physical body, it is
raised a spiritual body'. In time, it came to be supposed
that body and soul were separated—(the body in its grave,
the soul in a place of rest) until 'on the resurrection

morning', as the hymn says, 'soul and body meet again'—
on one great resurrection morning for all mankind. Meanwhile theology goes carefully on trying to trace a continuity of existence between the outworn physical body
and a spiritual body, continuous with it in some sense,
with which the person is 'clothed upon'.

For us today it is necessary to make the word 'body'
readily intelligible. For us a man's body is the physical
possession of a spiritual person. I am not my body; I have a
body; my body does not have me. At death a person disap-
pears from his body; and what was his body corrupts or is
destroyed and ceases to exist. Christian belief is that the
person goes on into the future life. This is quite definitely
a departure from the biblical idea derived from Christ's
resurrection. Christ died and was buried in the body, the
Father raised him from the dead; and Christ thus raised
rose with his body. But that leaves us free to picture what
happens to we men differently. We can no longer suppose
that at a given moment in the future all humanity will rise
from the dead with their bodies: nor can we think in terms
of some temporary separation of soul and body, whatever
that might mean. It is the end of a person's partnership
with his body. He goes on alone, without it. Is this survival without the body or 'mere survival'? Certainly not.
From the moment a person is born he is held in life by the
Holy Spirit, the Lord and Giver of Life. As I believe, and
as I think we all must believe, at death the Holy Spirit does
not desert the person but holds him still in life and brings
him through death to the forecourts of the Eternal Kingdom of God. So believing, we are set free from any continuing link with the physical body and from the idea that
there must be a spiritual body taking over from but in
some sense continuous with the physical body. We can

think simply about the person—you, me, any of us—as going on through and beyond death *to* life because still held *in* life by the Holy Spirit, Christian and non-Christian alike.

And so we can the more clearly see the future life not in terms of existence but in terms of fulfilment, or perhaps of violent readjustment; not 'I shall still exist' but 'I shall find fulfilment'—or more precisely, 'I shall be led on from where I am to such a kind or degree of fulfilment as the grace of God may be able to achieve in me.' Will everybody be 'saved' in the end? My instinct as an old schoolmaster is to say 'don't ask silly questions!' A silly question is a question which has no possible answer and is yet put forward as though it should be taken seriously.

Once in a television interview I was asked 'Do you believe in a future life?'—and I replied 'Of course I do: it is only a kind of promotion'. Not a few people wrote to thank me, first for giving that kind of answer and then for giving it with such confidence. How can I be so confident? Because if I believe in Christ as calling us into the kingdom of God, and in God as Father to us, it is mere common sense to see in what I have said here the reality of the matter—each person finding fulfilment or rather facing a new stage or kind of fulfilment; or it may be, being rescued, or being given the chance of being rescued, from frustration and vanity: and all this of course through Jesus Christ our Lord.

For he is—the Judge? Is that the right word? St. Paul was a Jew, trained in Mosaic Law and Roman Law; and of course he pictured the scene after death in terms of Law Court procedure, trials, advocates, sentence, punishment, acquittal. On the other hand Jesus Christ gives his picture of the final judgement in the parable of the sheep and the goats: and judgement is not by process of law but by the nature of the kingdom of God and of the 'good' life. The King will say to the sheep, 'Come, O blessed of my Father, inherit the kingdom prepared for you from the foundation of the world'—and to the goats 'Depart from me, you cursed, into the eternal fire prepared for the Devil and all his angels.' It is a vivid picture, and we can see its essential sincerity. Of course it is only a parable; and by another parable we can say with equal sincerity that the goats are only lost sheep for whom Christ is searching. But at the heart of the parable is the truth that beyond death we meet Christ not so much as the Judge, but rather as the sympathetic Assessor—and he assesses each person by what he has shown himself to be in the activities of his earthly life and in relating us to the Spirit of the kingdom of God. In the kingdom the living principle is fulfilment, triumphant over the frustrations, self-imposed or imposed from outside, which beset every man or woman. St. Peter was so right to speak of the Living Hope to which, through the resurrection of Christ, Christians are born again. It is the hope of receiving our inheritance, that for which we are born—fulfilment of our personal existence out of and beyond all the frustrations of human life.

There is much more to be said of all this than I shall attempt to say: but I add two reflections. The hope thus set before us is universal in character; for everyone who looks at himself at all is aware of a constant sense of frustration and has a desire or the possibility of a desire of some sort and of some strength for a fulfilment beyond his power to achieve. Eternity is set in our hearts. And secondly, if one is really aware of the kingdom of God and of its promise, one is also constantly observing in the activities of other persons glimpses of timeless goodness, beauty, truth which declare the reality of the kingdom of God, foretastes of the kingdom of God because they are themselves fulfilments. Jesus Christ in the parable of the sheep and the goats mentioned some, perfect fulfilments because done directly to one of the last of his brethren. There are so many other evidences of timeless and eternal moments made visible to those who have eyes to see them, tangible to those who can for a fleeting moment touch them, and all to the glory of God in his kingdom. Thus we can cease to argue with the agnostic about whether there was a physical resurrection of Christ or not. There was, as the New Testament says: but if anyone can't believe it— 'circumspice'. Use your eyes and see in every person some traces of that Spirit of Christ which he reveals to all who believe in him or in it and which brought him inevitably to his resurrection. 'God raised him up . . . because it was not possible for him to be held by death.'[1]

[1] Acts of the Apostles ch. 2, verse 24 from St. Peter's speech on *the* Day of Pentecost above all others.

5

Personal Efficiency

So we are liberated, from the selfish enquiry whether or no there is a future life, into the liberty of the kingdom of God. One cannot properly call our knowledge of that kingdom 'truth' because we know nothing about what it will be like to live in. Poets can rightly try to put into words their ideas of what it will be like. When Church authorities try to define conditions there or assign places in it, they cannot be right. We cannot attempt to get beyond our Lord's statement that some of the first here will be last there and some of the last here will be the first there—and how splendid a truth that is. But the fact of the kingdom, the prospect of fulfilment in God's kingdom, travels with us through life as a constant protection against fears and frustrations and ready at call to overthrow all spiritual adversaries and to arm us against physical pains and perils. And along with this Christian confidence goes another, the constant sense of handling, or the constant call to handle, our lives well; that is to say the urge, first in most of us natural and then a necessary part of Christian dedication, to be ourselves up to the best that we are capable of, efficient according to the measure of our faith and personal gifts.

We live at a time when people are very largely judged by (and paid by) their efficiency: but it is efficiency of a particular kind, dependent upon efficient application of a technical 'know how'; and that technique has to be mastered by people, and its possession registered by degrees and certificates, before anyone can be appointed to a recognised post or job. It is very true that for any job or profession, a man or woman must possess in some degree the skill or craftsmanship which goes with the job. I remember a television discussion on 'Why Education?', to which a number of students were contributing their rather frothy generalisations and which led in the end nowhere: but in the course of it an Oxford professor made a single contribution which was the only solid and sensible thing said. In university teaching, he said, there was the teacher and the pupil and 'the discipline of the subject matter'. To that, he said, both teacher and pupil must render respect and due obedience. Without that, there can be no efficiency but only wishful thinking (utopianism, idealism, idleness), or wearisome regret (despondency, indifference), or the futilities of remonstrance, rebellion and violent opposition. In attaining any degree of efficiency in any department of human skill there is a peculiar satisfaction. This sense of satisfaction is certainly of the kingdom of God. Any schoolmaster knows how a pupil may be 'redeemed' into life from mere passivity by the sudden discovery that he can do a thing well or that he wants to do a thing well or even that his master believes that he can begin to do a thing well. But satisfaction is only justified when it conforms to a discipline of the subject matter and for the Christian the subject matter is Christ's conception of God, man and the world. For personal efficiency in any job something more is needed over and above professional or technical efficiency.[1] The Christian

[1] Is there an age of pelagianism to be seen here? If we take enough trouble, we can save ourselves (and civilisation?) by our own efforts and efficiency. Pelagius was no fool. All good gifts we receive from God. But we have to direct them to God's ends in obedience to the discipline of the subject matter. Students in revolt may be full of good or bad idealisms: but as students they are neglecting the discipline of being a student.

knows that this 'something more' is derived from some kind of faith in the kingdom of God from which through the historic Christ and the ever present Holy Spirit each person possesses and is possessed by the twin dynamic forces—that of reaching out for a living fulfilment and that of achieving a living efficiency, and both to the glory of God.

I must try in a few words to indicate what I mean by living efficiency. Taught by Christ, the Christian knows that God is love. 'Faith, hope, love, there abide these three; but the greatest of these is love.' So said St. Paul in a famous passage. But it is almost impossible to confine to words what is meant by Love. It really means everything, since God is Love; and yet it can so easily be reduced in effect to meaning nothing beyond (as I once heard it put) 'a faint pink smell'. Once, in a padre's house with a group of young soldiers who were asking me questions, the problems of sex were raised. A very aggressive and scornful young boy said, in a context easy to imagine, 'If you love the girl, why shouldn't you?' What is the best quick answer to that? Having been a schoolmaster, I knew that in extremities the right thing is to attack, not to defend. So I said at once, 'My dear sir, have you any idea what love means?' A risky reply since it invites a counter-question, which I got—'Well, what does it mean?'. Without premeditation, and for the first time in my life, I replied at once, 'Don't you really know that Love means nothing apart from Responsibility?' Well, that silenced him. He knew that he had been answered fairly but knew also that the answer was out of his class of intelligence. It was only later that I came to realise that in an emergency I had come to utter a profound truth about God.

'God is love.' That is a 'word' about God. St. John, in the Prologue to his Gospel, goes on to say 'And the Word became flesh and dwelt among us, full of grace and truth: we have beheld his glory, glory as of the only Son from the Father . . . and from his fullness have we all received, grace upon grace.' God is love, and Jesus Christ Incarnate is our witness to the fact that God's Love was from the beginning made substantial in the reality of God's Word, his sense of Responsibility, who from the beginning was with God and was God. And then in time God so loved the world, that he sent his Son into the world to reveal the reality of God's love, the reality of his sense of responsibility and to call all who could believe in him to respond consciously both to God's love and to God's responsibility. And the reality of our response is shown in the degree in which we order or try to order our lives efficiently; both in doing this and that and in being the kind of person who is skilful (at least in intention) in the affairs with which we have to concern ourselves, and aiming also to be efficient in the things which pertain directly to the kingdom of God.

It remains for each one of us in his own experience and, as St. Paul says, 'according to the measure of his faith' to apply it to his own manner of living, being careful to see that whatever skills we may possess or lack, the only skill which has ultimate value or supramundane value is skilfulness in the values or virtues of the kingdom of God which can only be measured in terms of love operating responsibly.

There I leave this topic for the present. The inescapable fact is that it must be worked out by each person for himself or herself, in terms of love checked by its response to life, by the responsibility evoked. That is a personal search.

As St. Peter said, 'As God who has called you is holy, so must you be holy in all your daily conduct.' And almost every epistle of the New Testament ends with practical advice on daily conduct. There remains, of course, the fearful, exacting, merciless, exciting and often deeply satisfying problem of relating personal standards of moral conduct (holiness in itself) to the practical necessity of living with—and for—other people, other groups, other communities with other standards of moral conduct, of efficient living, of fulfilment, personal and social. Here I deliberately confine myself to the initial question which confronts every thinking person; and I say confidently that each of us who looks to Christ and the kingdom of God is lifted up thereby to seek such spiritual fulfilment and such efficient living as he is capable of.

6

Persons

BEFORE we go any further, we must ask what is meant by personal fulfilment, by personal efficiency; in fact, what is meant by a person. In its ultimate form the question is— who am I? But it is better to begin with the more general question—who and what is a person?—though we can never forget that every generalisation must sooner or later be tested by being faced with the particulars which it tries to reduce to a generality. What, then, is a person?

Some time ago, I have read, a university professor wrote an article in which he argued that the scientist must now be recognised as exercising those powers over human history which were formerly supposed to belong to God. I do not suppose that this professor believes in a personal God and Father or indeed in any knowable God. So what he was doing was to put the scientist onto the throne from which, as he thinks, God has been excluded. I would rather leave the throne vacant, than put any men, scientists or not, onto it. In the Acts of the Apostles it is said that 'All the Athenians and the foreigners who lived there spent their time in nothing except telling or hearing something new': and St. Paul, passing along in the city, and observing the objects of their worship found also an altar with this inscription, 'To an unknown god.' The discoveries and skills of modern science are indeed immense in their telescopic and in their microscopic significance, in their beneficent and in their unbeneficial possibilities and actualities. But no responsible scientist claims for himself or for his science absolute truth. He knows only too well that all his science is conjoined with the limitations of knowledge, from which no human being, nor humanity in the lump, can ever escape. But though that be true, it may be thought that natural science can at least reduce the human person to his constituent molecules or genes and chromosomes, and can even hope, having so reduced him, to find out how to put him together again, so becoming in some sense the creator of man. But even that is not to take the place of God. For science has to start from the given data, the subject matter of its studies. It cannot create them. It may discuss how a person's body and mind is put together and might one day find out how to make a fertilised human cell live and begin to grow in a test tube. If in the end the scientist could produce a viable person, he would have done with immense skill, labour and expense only what he has learned to do from studying God's handiwork, and using his materials. God has been doing just that same thing from the beginning in a much more business-like way.

No doubt a person is largely a product of his original genes and his subsequent environment; and it is a great help in dealing with unsatisfactory persons to know something about the 'somology' and 'psychology' of the person. But it is stupid not to take into account also his 'pneumology'. And when you have added together theologies of body, soul and spirit, you have still not explained the living person—Me or You.

In fact we must start with the particular in its own right and then one need not be alarmed at any kind of generalisation. That is just what an Oxford professor has recently done in a book called *The Glory of Man*.[1] It is not an easy book for the ordinary man: of course not. It is written in the language of modern scientific thinking. But it starts from the human person and finds the explanation of him and the substantial guarantee of his real value by the link between him and the person of Jesus Christ, and so finds the fulfilment of all personality in the kingdom of God.

We can now have the humility and common sense to take Jesus Christ at his own word. He talked to and about persons, from his Father down to the least of his brethren of the human family. He spoke little in generalities; he spoke much to persons inciting them to think, telling them what to do and telling them whom to admire as blessed or wise or competent. When he 'rebuked' Scribes and Pharisees it was not for knowing too little or too much, but for human stupidities in their use of their knowledge

[1] David Jenkins, SCM Press (London, 1967).

whereby they came under condemnation as hypocrites or 'whited sepulchres'.

There is a passage in St. John's Gospel (though it seems it was not part of his original gospel) in which a woman who had been caught in the act of adultery was brought to him by accusing Scribes and Pharisees. What would Jesus as a 'teacher' say about this case? They said quite correctly that by the Law of Moses she should be stoned to death. Jesus did not dispute the law, but said two things of a very personal nature. To the Scribes and Pharisees he said 'Let him who is without sin among you throw the first stone at her.' When all had gone except the woman he said 'Where are they? Has no one condemned you?'. When the woman said, 'No one, Lord', Jesus replied, 'Neither do I condemn you: go and do not sin again.'

When Jesus was on the Cross, there were crucified alongside him two thieves. One said to Jesus, 'Are you not the Christ. Save yourself and us.' He got no answer from Jesus. The other said, 'Jesus, remember me when you come in your kingdom.' To him Jesus replied, 'I tell you today you will be with me in Paradise.' The second thief knew little indeed about the kingdom to which he referred. He had not shown any personal efficiency in his past record. There was little, presumably, in him calling for fulfilment. But the answer Christ gave him was from a living person to a living person (I; you; me), even though both were next door to death, and he promised fulfilment in the kingdom of God.

To the Athenians Paul said, 'What, therefore, you worship as the unknown, this I proclaim to you.' Jesus Christ claims in his own person to show us the Father. He treats everyone as a person. So all who believe in him, believe in God as Father and believe in their own personal potentiality, as of one family in Christ.

We must use generalisations in our thinking as convenient summaries of a multitude of particular instances. But we can easily be deceived by them. For the problems which we have to face in life, whether we are Christians or not, are personal problems; and personal problems which lead so often to sorrow, suffering or strife can only be met and overcome by the intensely personal activities of sympathy and generosity. And sin is not a generalisation; nor is punishment, nor is forgiveness. All are intensely personal.

7

Sin

OF course, our next topic must be sin, a topic not to be regretted but welcomed as facing an inescapable fact of the human scene. The word itself needs careful watching. It is an abstract word, used to cover all forms of spiritual disorder in men just as disease is an abstract word, used to cover all forms of bodily disorder in men. Both forms of disorder must be analysed and investigated if they are to be made amenable to treatment, though every patient remains not a 'case' but a person. Ministers (whether of the Christian or of the medical profession) are men or women trained and certified as qualified and authorised by some competent body to deal with these disorders, spiritual or bodily as the case may be: and in fact neither can minister in his own profession effectively without some understanding of the skills of the other profession. In every society of men some disorders, whether spiritual or bodily, are endemic, some from time to time are epidemic. It is possible by a process of generalisation and speculation to speak of corporate sin and disease as belonging to the *corpus* of mankind; or as St. Paul does, to speak of cosmic sin and disease, the whole creation groaning in travail. But for our daily business and purposes, each one of us is concerned first with his own personal sin and disease; and the professional men, trained in the generalities, have to deal with each person in his own particularity with a positive desire to keep him in health or to restore him to health. In the records which we have of Jesus Christ in his teaching and actions, he appears far more interested in persons than in any general laws; he treated each case as a person to be delivered from his burden of sin or disease and to be restored to spiritual health. It is a simple fact of history that for reasons easy to understand the Christian Church has devoted far more of its general spiritual energies to denouncing sins and sinners than to the recreative work of overcoming evil by the divine power of good health. But each Christian, facing the problems of sin in himself and in society, must think first always, and with thanksgiving, that though there be no health in us the great gift of Christ which he offers to every man is a saving health, and a victory over the tyrannies of sin and death.

In general, everything which falls short of God's perfection is in some sense sin: but for our purposes here, we must think chiefly of the personal aspects of sin and leave the generalities to look after themselves. The verb is more important than the abstract noun, 'I sin' than 'sin'. Indeed sin has no meaning apart from sinners—and God. For the only yardstick by which sin can be measured and judged securely and consistently is that of the kingdom of God, and God's righteousness seen through the life of Christ. As persons we sin when in our own persons, wittingly or unwittingly, we depart from or fail to achieve the perfect will of God. Jesus Christ tells us not to judge others because we and they are all under the same judgement by God, and no one of us can tell what is in the heart of anyone else. Only of Jesus Christ can it be said, as is said in St. John's Gospel, that he knew what was in the hearts of men and needed no man to tell him.

Now this is splendidly clear. Jesus Christ shows us the way into the kingdom of God and leads us into it, saying 'Follow me'. He has shown us the way, he has declared something of the will of God our Father. He gave a promise, which every faithful disciple finds fulfilled in himself, that God the Holy Spirit would bring within our reach (as we daily need them) the things of God and would be ready to guide us into all truth. Each Christian can believe that according to the measure of his faith he is 'Spirit-filled' or 'Spirit-possessed', or to use another word 'sanctified', walking in the way of holiness—as well as of truth and love. It is up to each hearer to do his best and there are not a few 'means of grace' to help us along. It is in that context that the Christian looks at sin as a disorder which in the realm of spiritual efficiency spoils his own level of performance and in the realm of spiritual fulfilment robs him of some of the joys of fulfilment which might be his, distorting his view of the kingdom of God which is his appointed goal. Sin comes in, with and without his connivance, to spoil his Christian service of its perfect freedom. That is our condition, not to be bemoaned, not to be resented, not to be afraid of but to be cheerfully accepted with full sympathy for those who for one reason or another find the conditions of this service harder and heavier than they can bear or (it may be) than they are spiritually, or physically or mentally equipped to bear. We can at once see that the word 'sin' in them and in us covers a multitude of wrong thinkings or doings, not all of the same degree of culpability either in the abstract or in relation to the sinner concerned. Thus we can see at once the difference between sins of stupidity (not knowing what should be done), sins of clumsiness (knowing, but lacking the skill to do it well), sins of malice (proceeding from ill will against other men or against things in general or against God), sins of divided attention, or more often than not sins just of weakness of one kind or another. Every Christian should know enough of himself to be able to analyse his sins and his brother's in this kind of way. It will make him better able to criticise himself and to reform himself in co-operation with the Holy Spirit; it will make him better able to help others by his sympathy, and will make his prayers to the Father through Jesus Christ our Lord more intelligent. It will give direction to his prayers, for himself, for other men and for companies of people. It will make all his thoughts of sin sensible and sympathetic and will enable him to understand better what is meant by forgiveness.

8

Forgiveness

WE are moving still in the regions of spiritual reality and of spiritual experience opened up for us by Jesus Christ and by his witness to the eternal kingdom of God and to God himself as Father as well as King. All men from the beginning of man's recorded history have been conscious of and afraid of sin though unable to analyse its true meaning, and very often sin meant offending against the ritual of worship or just offending against the unknowable will of an arbitrary and hostile deity. So came the universal human desire to placate someone or something; to placate some 'It' or 'Them' in order to be delivered from the 'wrath to come' by pestilence or famine or some other disastrous manifestation of the deity's displeasure. In the context of the revelation of Jesus Christ, we can reach a reasonable understanding both of sin and of sin's forgiveness. For him and for us the sinner is the centre of concern; and the sinner must present himself in person before God who alone can judge the degree or nature of the sinner's culpability and who alone can award punishment or forgiveness—though we do not forget that Jesus Christ claimed for himself also during his ministry on earth the power to forgive sins. There is no room left here for supposing that God, like some human overlord jealous of his rights and authority, will decide by any arbitrary decision to punish a nation, a generation, a group, a household, even me for sins committed against his will or his law. Of course, as we saw earlier, there is the *discipline of the subject matter* for which God as creator is ultimately responsible and to which God, being reasonable, is as much subject as we his reasonable children are. Violations of that discipline which is a salutary part of our human condition must always bring unwelcome, distressing or disastrous consequences in their train. The scientist may be complete master of his own skill in his own subject matter; but the subject matter of science is not that of the spiritual condition of men, of men in their relation to the unseeable, unmeasurable God. But it is for the community to bring the results of scientific discovery before the judgement seat of society, along with the results of other skilled workers in other departments of knowledge—in many of which the subject matter is less amenable to precise measurement in the valuation than is that of the scientist. The community must preserve the right to say occasionally to the scientist: 'You can do this, no doubt—but you shall not do it here.' In the days of man's ignorance that would have been blind tyranny: but not so now. Our trouble is not that we know too much but that our knowledge is increasing so rapidly that we're often not very sure whether we want to use it or not. Men, we must never forget, are highly complex beings—animals, social animals, spiritual animals, conscious of their relative freedom of spirit, by nature rebellious against any attempt to restrain their freedoms and against any authority which claims to fulfil the duties of a father over a wayward child, rebellious against the discipline of the subject matter, reluctant to recognise God or to admit any authority of God. Men accordingly, even when aware of the disorders of man's making, are unwilling to accept any share of responsibility for them and, needing no forgiveness for themselves, are unwilling to forgive one another. They regard the idea of divine forgiveness as at best a confession of human weakness and at worst a piece of bogus psychology.

The Christian does not doubt that in his own person and as a member of society, knowing the good news of the kingdom of God and seeking to live in its spirit, he must always be ready to say and eager to say for himself and all men 'Lord, I have sinned against thy kingdom and before thee: we are no longer worthy to be called thy children'. Does the Christian at once add 'Lord, have mercy: Christ, have mercy: Lord, have mercy'? In his forms of corporate worship, perhaps: but even there, he knows the better way of which St. John speaks: 'If we confess our sins, he is faithful and just to forgive us our sins and to cleanse us from all unrighteousness.' The Christian community is a community of the forgiven: and we must in honesty add that if the Christian is to confess the sin he needs not only a broken and a contrite heart but also a sufficient understanding of what he means by sin. Then indeed God forgives at once. This is clearly part of the good news of the gospel. How can we be so confident? Only if this confidence has its origins and strength in the teaching of Jesus Christ.

Jesus Christ in his public ministry seems to be interested primarily in teaching his hearers to do the will of his heavenly Father and by being shining lights of that will to help others. Of course when he came across sins of society, he denounced them in no measured terms. 'Woe to you, Scribes and Pharisees, hypocrites.' Persons grouped in a society, in a profession, even in a Church can be subjected to a group condemnation, with more or less of justice. But the group cannot win forgiveness. Forgiveness is always in essence from person to person. Jesus Christ when speaking to or of sinners as persons, does so in personal terms and his forgiveness is easily given, almost anticipating any verbal confession of the sin. So it is in the parable of the Prodigal Son (to the displeasure of his elder brother). So it is in the parable of the publican who praying in the Temple says only 'Lord, be merciful to me a sinner', and is justified rather than the Pharisee with his very different (though not necessarily inaccurate) prayer. To the Woman taken in Adultery, Jesus said: 'neither do I condemn you: go, and do not sin again.' This was surely in effect a word of forgiveness, with all the recreative and remedial power that belongs always to forgiveness. The dying thief did not know much about sin in general or about his own sin in particular: but he knew enough, and to his death-bed repentance Jesus also on his death-bed made answer, 'Truly, I say to you, today you will be with me in Paradise.' It is not quite 'thy sins be forgiven thee': but that is what it means.

I once heard a preacher, speaking of forgiveness, distinguish between the *forgivingness* of God, (his quick readiness to forgive), the *forgivability* of us as sinners (our readiness not so much to deserve forgiveness as to understand what it means and requires on both sides) and the *forgiveness* which is such a very real part of Christian experience. By faith we know, and for certain, that God is a forgiving God and that all our daily Christian confidence rests on the fact that we are forgiven without any question of deserving it. It is not because we trust at all in ourselves or in our laborious efforts to make penitence more than a word. It is just a certainty of faith in Christ because he is the kind of person we trust to the uttermost. He forgives and sends us back to the battlefront of daily life, more than ever aware that God is love and that both in God and in us love finds itself only in responsibility which means in loyal service. But as we say this, we cannot forget that while this be truth in terms of the kingdom of God, yet in Church and State it is the duty of men of official authority or social influence, Christian or not, to judge their fellow men in objective terms of acquittal or condemnation, of reward or punishment. We cannot avoid that problem and must return to it presently.

9

Freedom and Authority

THERE is no doubt that those who saw or heard Jesus Christ in action regarded him as bringing them good news, a Gospel—a message about the kingdom of God. This message brought to them above all freedom and hope. So St. Paul said later to Christians that 'Christ has set us free'. St. Peter bids his hearers 'live as free men': and St. James speaks of the perfect law, the law of liberty. So in the Church of England Book of Common Prayer we address God daily thus:

> O God, who art the author of peace and lover of concord, in knowledge of whom standeth our eternal life, whose service is perfect freedom . . .

There could not be a better summary of the Christian Gospel. But as this generation knows to its cost, freedom is not enough by itself. It can only bear fruit, it can only bring forth good fruit, if it is subject to some authority. Without an authority, internal or external or so far as possible both, freedom is only another word for anarchy and nihilism. Jesus Christ preached a kind of freedom which can only exist in its plenitude in the kingdom of God, under God's direct authority: and in preaching the reality and finality of that kingdom, Jesus Christ claimed for himself full authority. The people who heard him saw that at once. 'The crowds were astonished at his teaching, for he taught them as one who had authority, and not as the scribes.'

John the Baptist in his prison wondered about him and sent disciples of his to question his authority. To them Jesus replied as a proof of his authority: 'Go and tell John what you hear and see: the blind receive their sight and the lame walk, lepers are cleansed and the deaf hear, and the dead are raised up' (all the visible and material signs of spiritual authority), 'and the poor have good news preached to them. And blessed is he who takes no offence at me.' So in St. John's Gospel, Christ is reported as saying to the hesitant, something like: 'If you cannot believe in me, then believe in my works: in both you will see the marks of the kingdom of God, and of the Father who works in me.'

That is a claim to authority which no disciples of Christ, no Christian Church, can ever make—the claim to have the direct authority of the kingdom of God and of God the Father in all that is done. If that be the authority of Christ, no mortal man can prove it: Christ himself did not attempt to prove it. He asserted it as his by nature. Men must either recognise it or reject it—or in a way so usual and acceptable among men, both recognise it and reject it in a spirit of sincere and satisfactory compromise: or they may follow the example of the Athenians who heard Paul preach when 'some mocked, but others said—we will hear you again' to continue the discussion.

Scribes and Pharisees, lawyers and Herodians, all the representatives of constituted authority tried to disprove his authority by putting questions to him hoping to catch him out. At the end of one of these trials of strength, Jesus Christ turned the tables and put a question to his questioners—about authority. It is not a question that interests us, but touched them in a very tender spot since it concerned their chief theological principle, the Messiahship. Jesus Christ quotes at them a Psalm of David about the Messiah:

> The Lord said to my Lord
> Sit at my right hand,
> till I put thy enemies under thy feet.

'Here', says Jesus Christ, 'David inspired by the Lord God calls his son, the Messiah, *My Lord*; but how can the Messiah with all the divine authority of the Messiah be his son, subject to David's paternal authority?'—a very proper question to put to theologians and lawyers who claimed to know all the answers: and, says St. Matthew's Gospel 'No one was able to answer him a word, nor from that day did anyone dare to ask him any more questions'. As on another occasion Christ by a word 'declared all foods clean', so on this occasion he confounded the authority of the experts who pitted themselves against his own authority in the kingdom of God.

But he did not give us any reason to suppose that his authority can be always invoked in all human questions. The politicians asked him on one occasion whether it was right to pay tribute to Caesar or not, a question involving money. Where in these days he might well have said 'what is money?', he said 'show me a coin'—and then told them to use their brains honestly, 'Render to Caesar what is owed to his authority and to God what is owed to him'. There was a more startling question put to him by political humanitarians (or humanitarian politicians). Pilate's soldiers had caught some Galileans offering their animal sacrifices to God and they had slain them, mingling their blood with their sacrifices. What about that? Christ would not attempt to give a ruling on such a question of intermingled politics and humanitarianism and religious sentiment with all the controversy that must attach itself to any answer. He speaks therefore only of what relates to the kingdom of God and his authority therein. 'Do you think that these Galileans were worse sinners than all the other Galileans because they suffered thus? I tell you, No: but unless you repent you will all likewise perish'. So too, he adds, about the people killed in Siloam by a falling tower. He refuses to give a 'straight answer' about these catastrophes because, I imagine (and experience today confirms it), they cannot be answered in terms of the kingdom of God.[1] Men must use their common sense in dealing with them. The true answer is—Repent: think again in terms of the kingdom of God: that is the only way to come to terms with the brutalities of men or the accidents of fortune.

It is not to be doubted that Jesus Christ meant his disciples to establish his Church in the world to carry on his work of leading people to the kingdom of God. The Church would inevitably have to deal with this endless problem of the conflict between the free man and authority whether represented by a person, or by a collection of

[1] Thus it is to my mind wrong for churchmen to interfere as such in relation to details concerning purely political questions such as support of Nigeria in its recent civil war or to the war against world poverty and illiteracy or indeed to 'World Development'. They can do no more than give their personal opinions.

persons, or by a system of authority or by the discipline of the subject matter. It is an essential part of the Christian Gospel that the element of authority is provided by the kingdom of God and his righteousness and by Jesus Christ as its exponent. It is in this context and with these limitations that men must consider the Authority of the Cross, the authority of his crucifixion in his way back to the Kingdom from which he came and the authority of his resurrection.

IO

Long-suffering

JESUS Christ was the proclaimer of the kingdom of God and everything that he said or did was related to that kingdom. The record given in the four gospels makes it quite clear that Jesus knew from the start that to preach his gospel of the kingdom was to challenge and affront all who were committed to the ways of the world or had their possessions and their hearts there: and to challenge men's consciences in that way is always to incur hostility and invite suffering. He was prepared to face all the consequences of his own witness to the kingdom and had no doubt that beyond all possible mortal suffering lay the victorious certainty of the kingdom with its eternal livelihood. So it was that after St. Peter's confession of faith in him, he is recorded as saying: 'The Son of Man must suffer many things, and be rejected by the elders and chief priests and scribes, and be killed, and on the third day be raised'. He knew the kind of things that lay ahead for him: but he knew also that for anyone who tried to follow him into the kingdom there must be suffering too. 'If any man would come after me, let him deny himself and take up his cross daily and follow me. For whosoever would save his life will lose it; and whosoever loses his life for my sake will find it—for my sake and the gospel's will save it'.[1] In another passage he is recorded as saying 'Do not think I have come to bring peace on earth: I have not come to bring peace, but a sword . . . and a man's foes will be those of his own household. He who loves father or mother more than me is not worthy of me . . . and he who does not take up his cross and follow me is not worthy of me', and immediately afterwards 'Whosoever gives to one of these little ones even a cup of cold water because he is a disciple, truly, I say to you, he shall not lose his reward.' Acceptance of suffering and compassion for sufferers go hand in hand. 'Come to me, all who labour and are heavy-laden: and I will give you rest. Take my yoke upon you and learn from me; for I am gentle and lowly in heart and you will find rest for your souls. For my yoke is easy, and my burden is light.' To all sufferers he offered the compassion of a fellow sufferer for the kingdom and the assurance of a victory to be achieved.

When his own hour of supreme trial drew near, he made a prayer in Gethsemane: 'My father, if it be possible, let this cup pass from me: nevertheless, not as I will, but as thou wilt'. As he prayed, he knew that what was about to happen was inevitable in the world of men to which he had come, an inevitable part of his witness to his own gospel.

[1] St. Mark's Gospel adds 'and the gospel's' to the 'for my sake' of St. Matthew's and St. Luke's Gospels.

Pontius Pilate was perhaps one of the few who had a glimmering of what was in Christ's mind as he faced his end. When the Jewish authorities had condemned Jesus to death and came to Pilate as Governor to confirm the sentence, Pilate, according to St. John, did what must have been an exceptional thing. He returned to the pretorium again and summoned Jesus and questioned him about the charge that he claimed to be King of the Jews. The brief conversation that followed is of absorbing interest. In reply to a question Jesus said something like this, 'You ask whether I am a king. My kingship is not of this world. But you are right: I am a King. That's why I came into this world to bear witness to the truth'. And Pilate said to him, 'What is truth?' Did he say it in a hurry, not staying for an answer? I doubt it. He knew that he had his governor's duty to perform and he could not delay it. His 'What is truth?', as I see it, was to bring this unusual conversation to a close with a question that left the question unresolved. But he expressed his feelings not long after when he said to the Jews bluntly—'What I have written, I have written'—King of the Jews. I was once asked, in the middle of a Naval Review at the time of the Queen's coronation, by a Middle East Sheik 'was Pilate a good Governor or a bad one?' He had seen an American film of the life of Christ, and this was the question which excited a professional interest in him. A good Governor? Yes, since he was there in Jerusalem to keep this turbulent people in order, and not to provoke them to violent protest and most likely to violence: and since the Jewish courts had condemned Jesus on religious grounds, he should not refuse to confirm their judgement. A good Governor? What is good? What is truth? So Christ was crucified. For what purpose? To what end? The Church has been trying to explain the meaning of the Atonement from that day to this and has never satisfied itself with its answers, and for a very good reason. No generalisation suffices. Each man and woman must find his or her own answer, meeting his or her own burden, his or her own share in the burdens of other people and of the world by such understanding as he has of Christ and of his passion and of his kingdom—and his degree of understanding may be for many undefined and undefinable or may find refuge in familiar words of a hymn or of scripture or in music or in musical words. That is as it should be.

What did Christ himself say about his crucifixion? 'I, if I be lifted up (on the cross) will draw all men unto me.' That is still the truth. Churchmen must be terribly careful lest by their much talking and deep devotion they cause the Cross to repel men rather than attract them and so obscure the fact that the Cross and all it stands for is a terrible but essential part of Christ's winning through to his resurrection, and so has its place in every victory of the Spirit and of the kingdom of God in the hearts of men.

II

Christian and Churchman

THERE is no doubt that in the first days of the Church recorded in the Acts of the Apostles and the books following in the New Testament, the words Christian and churchman were regarded as synonymous. A convert to Christ was at once baptised into Christ and so into his Church. On the first day of Pentecost St. Peter's words to enquirers who had heard his message was 'Repent and be baptised', and so 'those who received his word were baptised and there were added that day about three thousand souls'.

Once on a Sunday in Detroit Cathedral, I looked into one of the classrooms and found a class of boys and girls aged about 12 or 13 at work. I asked the teacher what they were studying and was told 'religion'—just that! The next thing was that a girl put a question to me—Do you have to be baptised to be a Christian? My answer must clearly be immediate and precise. I said: You can be a Christian without being baptised: but to be a churchman you must be baptised. My answer departed from New Testament standards: but it is, I think, what must be said and accepted everywhere today.

Christ revealed the kingdom of God in his ministry and laid open the way of life by which men and women can even now begin to live according to the ways of the kingdom of God after his example and in the sure and certain hope of entry into it beyond death. Practically all we can claim to know about the Gospel which Christ preached and lived is contained in the four gospels of the New Testament, four accounts by disciples of what the Church remembered and could record. So far we have been considering a few of the main themes of the gospel which Christ preached. No one can catch a true idea of the Christian way of life except by reading and re-reading the gospel accounts. But some ideas of it have passed into common knowledge in most countries, and are widely accepted as necessary to a reasonable and decent way of living and to a civilised society. Thus there are those who if asked their religion might say 'I accept as my religion the sermon on the mount'. They may be a long way from understanding the real meaning or the full meaning of this as a confession of faith; but it would be difficult to deny that it is in some sense a confession of a Christian faith, a recognition that in some sense Christ can claim to be the Light of the World. And even in such a casual confession of an inarticulate faith, there is some sense of endeavour, some element of hope, some acceptance of long-suffering and sacrifice, some dedication to compassion and neighbourliness, some feeling after an eternal kingdom of God which is not to be found in the same way in a non-Christian person or society or nation.[1]

The Church should be happy and thankful to recognise that this kind of attitude is not to be denied the name of Christian. Where it is found, we rightly thank God for it. Without it the Church would have nothing to build on. In fact this Christian attitude is to be found in many who

---

[1] Is this humanism? No. Humanism is a system of thought concerned with human (and not divine) interests, and with the interests not of the individual but of mankind. 'Christian humanism' is a contradiction in terms. All Christians must be concerned both with humanity (the human race and human nature) and with men in their individuality because of the person of Christ and the doctrine of his Incarnation.

would not call themselves Christian or who have never heard of Christ's kingdom. They too are not necessarily far from the kingdom of God. To the Church Christ committed the task of continuing his work, of preaching the kingdom of God, of living according to its way, of bringing men to the kingdom. To be a churchman is to be involved, initially by Baptism, in the message and mission of the Church.

In this first part I have tried to indicate the foundation on which the Church must build. In part two I consider the Church in history.

PART TWO:
THE CHURCH OF CHRIST

12

From Kingdom to Church

THE kingdom which Jesus Christ preached and lived, from which he 'came' and to which he 'returned' is without limits or boundaries, beyond all regulation, definition or rules. It is the kingdom of God; as he is Spirit, so his kingdom is spiritual. He desires to share his kingdom with all Christian people, and indeed with all men. In a sense all men are already within the embrace of that kingdom—since we cannot be men and be outside it. And again, in a sense, we can call God's kingdom the spiritual realm of good manners and of ideas, good as God alone is good. When an enquirer greeted Jesus Christ as Good Master, Jesus said, 'Why do you call me good? No-one is good but God alone.' What Jesus Christ did for mankind was to establish among men the saving truth of the kingdom of God; and anyone who has some kind of faith in this truth is some kind of Christian. It does not matter that much whether my attempt in part one, to indicate the nature of the kingdom is right or wrong, sufficient or insufficient. Anyone can read the gospels for himself. There is the record, the only record the Church has, of what Christ told his disciples and the world about that kingdom.

In the period between Easter Day and Ascension Day, as we are told in the Acts of the Apostles, Jesus Christ presented himself alive to his apostles by many proofs and talked to them of the kingdom of God. It was under his direction and impulse and authority that as witnesses to

Christ they presented his Church on the stage of history, on a 'day of Pentecost', which we call Whit Sunday.

Unlike the kingdom, the Church, in order to be the Church, must have limits and boundaries, constitution, regulations and rules like any other human society since to outward view it is a human society. As its name 'ecclesia' indicates, the Church is an assembly—a society of persons called out of the general public and into a special association or fellowship, belonging as the word Church indicates, to the Lord, to our Lord Jesus Christ.[1] The Church of Christ must have ministers of his Word and Sacraments with authority in his Church. The Church can never *be* the kingdom; it can only bear witness to it by its own exhibition of good Christian manners and good Christian ideas; and in the Church, as St. Paul once said, every member is both a spiritual man and a man of flesh, and all are at various stages of growth in Christ from babyhood to maturity. Every member of the Church, as being a spiritual man, has his own powers of judgement and his own authority, and is 'himself to be judged by no man'. Yet, as St. Paul in his own building of the Church showed clearly enough, there must be authority or authorities in the Church to deal with matters of behaviour and of ideas about God, Christ, the Church and mankind.

There are some churchmen who resent the churchly condition of the Church of Christ and want to lead the whole Church into some kind of spiritual plenitude and structural unification here on earth. Surely they are avoiding the plain discipline of the subject matter. The Church must accept the fact that it has the gospel of the kingdom in its own earthly ecclesiastical vessels, with their

[1] The word Church or Kirk is derived from a Greek word (*kuriake*) meaning belonging to the Lord. The Kyries = the Kuries, the 'O Lords'.

own limitations of constitution and diversities of ideas concerning administrative rule and regulation. What matters is that the Church in ministering Christ's Word and Sacraments through the churches shall manage its own affairs with grace, wisdom and understanding. But in order to discover what are its affairs, and how they are to be regarded it is necessary first to come to terms with the question—what is the Church?

13

The Church in General

CHURCH history as it has evolved and is evolving is a confusing and even a dangerous territory for all who travel through it. Each Church has its own map of the main roads, by-passes, side-roads and cross country tracks available for its members. We live at a time when, as churchmen of all the Churches have come to realise, ecclesiastical main roads are liable to get blocked; bridges over swampy ground are often unable to cope with all the traffic of modern knowledge, modern ideas, and modern manners and conditions; and many of the clergy and the laity find it more interesting and profitable to do their private walking across country by open moorlands or mountain, following such tracks as they find or making their own.

Critics and reformers whether churchmen or not speak to the world as though in the Church itself authority was out of date, church order unimportant, theology in a ferment of unknowing and all doctrine under sentence of death: and all this has a devastating effect on the general public and a depressing effect on the faithful laity (who are not as few as is sometimes supposed). The truth is that (to continue the former metaphor) a great work of ecclesiastical roadmaking and repair and restoring of rights of way is in hand throughout Christendom. At such a time Church loyalties may suffer: but twice blessed are they who do not forget that their loyalty to the Church community must always mean more to them than mere loyalty to their own ideas and that in all their loyalties they and the Church stand under the Judgement of God.

What we have received from and through Jesus Christ of the kingdom of God and of his Church is unshaken and indeed unshakable by men. The manner of its presentation and the arts of its communication have always been liable to get out of order and have always had to call for reformation. The author of the Epistle to the Hebrews was well aware of this situation. He was deeply involved in working out a theology of transition for some of his Jewish-Christian friends. His words to them are apt for today. 'Let us hold fast the confession of our hope without wavering, for he who promised is faithful; and let us consider how to stir up one another to love and good works, not neglecting to meet together, as is the habit of some, but encouraging one another'—and, I would add, the more so as we see the disciplines of good Christian manners and good Christian ideas being neglected. So let us consider what the Church is and is for.

By the Church we mean, in the first instance anyhow, the whole visible Church, the Church Militant here on earth. Its proper title, the Catholic Church cannot be used for this purpose without distracting explanations since to so many people, churchmen and others, it has come to mean only the Roman Catholic Church to the exclusion of all other Churches. It can very properly be referred to as the Universal Church: but that word lacks something of authority. It could be called the Oecumenical Church, the one Church of the inhabited world: but that word is not easily understood nor easy to say. Simplest is often best; and the least confusing usage is to refer to the whole Church of Christendom as the General Church, and to the Churches comprehended in it as particular Churches within the General Church. We may then without confusion say that the General Church can be regarded metaphorically as a temple, a body, a bride of Christ (to mention some of the New Testament metaphors applied to it), or from another aspect as the Church Militant and from another as the Church Ministerial and as called at all times to be the Church Eirenic dedicated always to the Peace of God.

Throughout history, men of piety and imagination have sought to glorify the One Church of Christ by all the resources of mystical and metaphysical thinking and praying. Much of this has been good and of permanent value; and has brought refreshment of spirit and deepening of devotion to all the Churches: but parts of it have been or have become spiritually unhealthy, metaphysically confusing, imaginatively exaggerated. Such thinking always has its dangers in that it leads thought and devotion away from the rock whence we are all hewn to find our satisfaction in human speculation and imaginings. Thus the Church of England does not take kindly to the idea of giving to the Church the title of Mother Church since in sober fact the Church has none of the qualities of a mother, but is a society or association of persons supernaturally originated and sustained. The Church stands always in the context of the Incarnation of Christ and of history. We must always remember to think and pray in full awareness of the Church and of the Churches simultaneously. Thus, securely held to the realities of history each Church, while having its freedom to explore at will into the mystery of its apostolic calling and heritage, tries as best it can to give expression to the realities of the kingdom of God and his righteousness, uplifted to share with the whole company of heaven in one freedom, one servitude and one worship.

14

The One Church

CHRIST willed one Church and through the Holy Spirit the Apostles initiated the one Church as described in the second Chapter of the Acts of the Apostles. From the moment of its dramatic launching in Jerusalem it was the Universal or Catholic Church of Christ, Militant here on earth. Later on it gave itself the title of the One, Holy, Catholic, and Apostolic Church: but it has always been made manifest in and through particular Churches. We can only establish visible contact with the General Church through one or other of the particular Churches which are comprised in Christendom.

From the beginning until this very day, there have been two unique possessions by means of which the One Church is distinguished from all other Christian or non-Christian societies. One is the Sacrament of Baptism in the name of the Holy Trinity, the visible means by which persons are admitted and received into the visible Church. The other is its Creed in one or other of its forms as a symbol or summary of its Christian faith. A very early credal expression of this faith can be found in St. Paul's Epistle to the Ephesians:

> I therefore, a prisoner for the Lord, beg you to lead a life worthy of the calling to which you have been called, with all lowliness and meekness, with patience, forbearing one another in love, eager to maintain the unity of the Spirit in the bond of peace. There is one body and one Spirit, just as you are called to the one hope that belongs to your call, one Lord, one faith, one baptism, one God and Father of us all, who is above all and through all and in all.

In these words St. Paul suggests the three differentials of the Church Militant—Unity of the Spirit in one faith, unity of Church Order in the one body, and unity of endeavour in the leading of a life worthy of the Christian calling.

Later it was possible to differentiate the General Church more clearly by specifying on the one hand its possession of the two dominical sacraments of Baptism and the Lord's Supper and on the other the possession of the New Testament. The Sacraments constitute the permanent outward and visible evidence that the Church is essentially a supernatural body with its existence in the reality of the kingdom of God with Christ as its Head and the Holy Spirit as the giver of its life.[1] The New Testament binds it indissolubly to history and to the here and now in its account of the incarnate ministry of Christ and the ministry of his Word and Sacraments through the continuing body of his disciples, the fellowship of the baptised.

[1] It must be made clear at once that the Churches of Christ which make of the Sacrament of Baptism the initial act of admission are already in organic union with one another as being thereby within the structural organism of the body of Christ. Full Communion between these Churches brings them to a richer form of organic union.

15

The Churches

THE General Church with its simple structure based on baptism and the New Testament operates through the particular Churches: and each Church must have its own structure. Church history consists of the histories of the particular Churches in the General Church, of their collaborations and of their conflicts. Theologians speak of an undivided Church as once existing: but at no time was the General Church without divisions of one kind or another, territorial, doctrinal, constitutional, ethical, political.

Sir Steven Runciman in his book *The Great Church in Captivity*[1] writes:

> As the Church on earth grew in size, so it grew in divisions. The jealous rivalries of hierarchs, the interference and resentment of the laity, and the love of theologians to expose the damnable errors made by others of their craft have combined with differences in historical development and in spiritual temperament to break it into separate units; and even where cracks have been mended the line of the former breakage has always remained exposed. The most serious division in the mediaeval Church was that which came to separate its two most important branches, the great Church of Old Rome and the great Church of New Rome which is Constantinople and of her sister Patriarchates.

About a century after this, the Great Schism between East and West, came the Reformation which split the Western Church. Through all schisms and heresies the idea and the actuality of the One Church persisted even

---

[1] *The Great Church in Captivity* (Cambridge, 1968) p. 81.

while Churches disagreed as to the meaning of baptism or the interpretation of the New Testament. The One Church of Christ persisted, a united Church even in its hostile divisions. We live at a period when the existence of the unity of us all in that one Church is recognised again and is bearing much fruit. The task which is engaging the attention of most Churches is that of bringing into some kind of workable union of structure the different particular Churches. There are generally speaking three possible solutions. All the Churches might grow together and by a process of increasing unification become a Church of a single organisation, the unitary Church of Christ. Or one Church might be and remain the dominant Church, bringing all other Churches into union with it by sub-mission, the imperial Church of Christ. Or there is the way of the coming together of the autonomous Churches into a relationship of Full Communion with one another, the plural Church of Christ which is also and essentially the One Church of Christ.[1] We shall all, in the end, as I think, have to feel our way forward to the structural realisation of Full Communion: but first let us consider certain unities of the One Church which must be found also in all particular Churches, though since the Churches are very human societies as well as supernatural the unities will always be accompanied by disunities of spirit among their members.

[1] The idea of an ultimate unification of all Churches in a single structure was adopted without examination by many in the enthusiasm of the oecu-menical movement who confused unity of spirit and structural unity. In an article in *The Tablet* (March 7, 1970) Bishop B. C. Butler showed a keen interest (so far as I know, for the first time from the Roman Catholic side) in the idea of Full Communion between the Church of Rome and the Anglican Communion, though combining it with a preservation in theory of the Church of Rome as the dominant Church of Western Christendom.

16

Unity of the Spirit

ST. Paul called the Ephesians to maintain unity of the Spirit in the bond of peace. If the Churches of Christendom are to be in any visible sense united, there must be certain unities, unity of the one Spirit, unity of doctrine, unity of Church order, unity of operation and unity of moral outlook, by which I mean common ideas of holiness or righteousness or customary ethics. I begin with the first named—Unity of Spirit.

In my first chapter I mentioned a prayer from the Book of Common Prayer for the Catholic Church which puts together in one sentence the way of truth, unity of spirit, the bond of peace, righteousness of life. In the Communion service, similarly, we pray that the Universal Church may be inspired with the spirit of truth, unity and concord and may agree 'in the truth of thy holy Word and live in unity and godly love'. St. Paul writing to the Galatians gives a list of the works of the flesh including 'strife, jealousy, anger, selfishness, dissension, party spirit', saying that those who do such things shall not inherit the kingdom of God. By contrast, he goes on, 'but the fruit of the Spirit is love, joy, peace, patience, kindness, goodness, faithfulness, gentleness, self-control; against such there is no law'. All these qualities or virtues which Christians are called upon to display in their daily lives are gifts of the Holy Spirit, not self-originated but to be received and then by prayer and self-discipline to be trained and developed and brought towards perfection: and one of these gifts of the

Holy Spirit is unity. But in the particular context of Church Unity, this gift of the Holy Spirit stands apart from and above all other gifts of the Holy Spirit. It can be present with Christians even while they are properly differing about ways of truth and of righteousness and of many other things. It has its own blessing and bears its own fruit to the glory of God: and for that very reason Churches and churchmen must be ever on their guard against exploiting it for the furtherance of their own ideas or purposes. Christ said once 'where two or three are gathered together in my name, there am I in the midst of them'. Unity between Christians is always the sign of Christ's presence in their midst; but it cannot be invoked to stimulate interest in or support for programmes or propaganda concerned with man-contrived schemes however good.

St. John records in his Gospel the prayer of our Lord for Unity at the Last Supper in these words:

> I have manifested thy name to the men whom thou gavest me out of the world; thine they were, and thou gavest them to me and they have kept thy word . . . and now I am no more in the world, but they are in the world, and I am coming to thee. Holy Father, keep them in thy name which thou hast given me, that they may be one, even as we are one.

and later

> I do not pray for these only, but also for those who are to believe in me through their word, that they may all be one; even as thou, Father, art in me and I in thee, that they may also be in us, so that the world may believe that thou hast sent me. The glory which thou hast given me I have given to them, that they may be one even as we are one, I in them and thou in me, that they may become perfectly one, so that the world may know that thou hast sent me and hast loved them even as thou hast loved me.

So Christ has described for us what Unity of the Holy
Spirit means. It is a divine quality uniting Father and
Son and Holy Spirit. It is given by the Holy Spirit to persons, to Christ's first disciples and to those who believe in
Christ through their word. It is given without measure,
without nicely calculated less or more. It is surrounded by
glory and love. It may be there in its own power among
disciples one minute and gone the next. We live by its rays,
but we cannot control them by our calculations. It shines
through persons and personal acts only. Churches as such
cannot create unity of the Spirit. They can and should
provide an environment conducive to unity and should
teach their members to pray and live in the spirit of unity;
but if they try self-consciously to promote it, they may
easily fall into the delusions of self-deceit, and the errors
and cruelties of crowd pressures. It is an essential part of
love and unity that each participant maintains his or
her own separate identity. None of us should talk of
Church unity unadvisedly, lightly or wantonly, but
reverently, discreetly, advisedly, soberly, and in the fear
of God.

I have many times in my life been vividly aware of unity
made almost visible, a sure sign of Christ present with his
people—sometimes in oecumenical gatherings and worship, more often in gatherings of Church people of my
own or of other Churches, assembled for their own
domestic worship at which I have been present. A few
occasions stand out with a glory all their own—some of
the great services, the glorious united celebrations of the
Holy Communion in which I have been privileged to have
a place in many parts of the Anglican Communion, in
oecumenical gatherings or on some great scale at Lambeth
Conferences or in our home dioceses. Their true glory has

been not in their pomp and circumstance or magnitude but in the abounding grace of brethren so diverse in so many gifts sharing with one faith and one affection in the acts of prayer and worship, so for the moment made wholly one in the Divine Unity itself. But if there be one glory of such gatherings, there is an equal glory of gatherings on a far smaller scale, yet thereby endued with a special glory of their own, the grace of the intimate, the domestic, the small which I have known among church-men of many Churches in England, Wales, Scotland and Ireland; and especially dear to me have been little gather-ings in village churches, telling in their own language something specially lovely of the mighty works of God. Apart from all these and equally precious have been the continual and countless occasions when this divine unity has come to life among some two or three of us engaged together in some piece of honest Christian work, religious or secular, as a committee, in an enterprise, a discussion, in singing, or walking—whatever it may be when a radiance of happiness and holiness (which are really the same thing) shines upon us.

I wish here to relate a special experience of my own life. Shortly before I retired from my office as Archbishop, towards the end of the year 1960, of my own volition but prompted by many considerations, I made a short pilgrimage first to Jerusalem, then to Istanbul and then to Rome. Arriving in Jerusalem by air I was received by our Archbishop there and driven to our Cathedral Church of St. George. There were gathered the heads of all the Churches, Greek, Latin, Armenian, Coptic, Lutheran, Franciscan, White Fathers, all Christendom in miniature, there to welcome the Archbishop of Canterbury and to-gether we prayed and sang the Te Deum. Here was no thought of unions or intercommunions, no negotiations or counting of claims. The one great advantage that I had was that neither for myself nor for the Anglican Communion did I claim or want to receive anything at all beyond the gracious courtesies of the kingdom of God. But there in that Cathedral and later in a social gathering in its parish hall and in many other ways there was a visible representation of Christendom at unity in itself, a felt presence of the unity of the One Church of Christ, a fulfilment realised in experience.[1]

From there I went to Istanbul to meet again Athenagoras, the Oecumenical Patriarch, Head of the Orthodox Churches throughout the world; and from there to Rome to meet Pope John XXIII, a meeting of historic importance in that Pope and Archbishop of Canterbury had not met for nearly 500 years. Of these two visits, one to the Phanar to which the territorial rights of the Oecumenical Patriarch are now reduced, and the other to the Vatican State to which the territorial rights of the Pope are now limited, by startlingly and painfully different historical processes, I will say no more than this. In the Phanar I was able to enter, as always straightway, into participation with the Oecumenical Patriarch in the glory of an Orthodox celebration of the Divine Mysteries: in the Vatican the Pope in welcoming me, was disregarding all rules of protocol in the Vatican, and together we were breaking down barriers that have barred Roman Catholics and

---

[1] A Greek word for 'fulfilment' is *pleroma* and St. Paul speaks of it a good deal. He means by it the final spiritual fulfilment of God's whole purpose in God's good time, for which he chooses the words *telos* and *eschatan*. We must say now that any such fulfilment will so far as we can tell be outside our time, a vision not to be realised in our time, a spiritual reality not to become part of temporal history. Our Lord is recorded as saying on one occasion (Luke 18, 8) 'Nevertheless when the Son of Man comes, will he find faith on earth?'

Anglicans from Christian friendship for centuries. Structural barriers of doctrine and Church Order still divide the Greek, Roman and Anglican Communions: but they are of relatively small importance. Through them all the light of the Divine Spirit of Unity is shining and by them we are learning to walk together in Unity of Spirit. That light shone brilliantly on my visit to Jerusalem. It shone again in Jerusalem more brilliantly still when a few years later Pope and Oecumenical Patriarch met there and exchanged the Kiss of Peace.

17

Unity in Doctrine

EACH Church of the General Church is responsible for itself before Christ, and is the guardian of its own Christian doctrine. It will of course as part of its life in Christ encourage its members to be ever examining in the light of growing experience past definitions of doctrine and to be ever revitalising or refashioning them by new thinking and by newly perceived aspects of divine truth. In doing this its thinkers will be in touch with leaders of thought in other Churches: but each Church is its own master and must not allow adventurous thinkers or reformers to compromise its own integrity. Here is the familiar problem of control. Freedom must not be stifled, authority must not be flouted, in matters of doctrine. The Church of England very wisely does not interfere unless it has to with its members' freedoms: and then more by a word of caution or advice than by any restraining or rebuking action. Thus, though there may be the appearance of disorder, the way is left open for free and friendly discussions of doctrine without disruptions of harmony or order except in so far as individuals or groups forget the spirit of unity and the demands of good manners. Otherwise responsible schools of thought learn to live in a peaceable tension with one another to their own mutual benefit and enrichment.

Perhaps the greatest discovery in Church relations in this century has been to find that separate Churches can live together in friendship and co-operation while each keeps its full freedom to retain and to amend its own particular doctrinal traditions, provided always and only that no one separate Church claims the right to judge or overrule another Church. In 1930 the Church of England found how to come into Full Communion with the Old Catholic Churches on the continent whose doctrinal background was very different. They found that there was sufficient doctrinal agreement in essentials to justify Full Communion, and (very wisely) no attempt was made to say what those essentials were, thus leaving to each Church its own doctrinal freedom, in secure mutual trust that each would so regard the other that all should be done to the edifying of the General Church in love.

The story of the Great Schism between the two predominant Churches of East and West provides an admirable object lesson.[1] The chief point of doctrinal conflict at the Council of Florence which preceded it was concerned with a purely metaphysical matter. Granted that the source of all godhead was in God the Father, and that the Son is of the Father alone (not made, nor created but

[1] What follows is mostly borrowed, I hope correctly, from Chapter 4 of Sir Steven Runciman's *The Great Church in Captivity*.

begotten, as the Athanasian creed says), and that the Holy Spirit is (in the words of the same creed) not made, nor created, nor begotten but proceeding, then, it may be asked, does the Holy Spirit proceed from the Father *through* the Son or from the Father *and* the Son? One can see the point. If *through* the Son, the Father remains the sole source of godhead; but if *from* Father and Son (the *filioque* clause) then Father and Son are linked together as joint sources of the godhead of the Holy Spirit. The West thought the difference trivial. Gibbon and many other historians have regarded the difference as 'inevitable and harmless'. Sir Steven Runciman says that the difference was more than a matter of words and was the expression of two opposing attitudes in religious thought. The fact is that to anybody except a metaphysician such a question of abstract speculation is without meaning and without interest. So far as I am a metaphysician, I am entirely on the side of the Greek divines: but as a student of unity in doctrine, I should say that each Church has full liberty to keep its own version of this trinitarian doctrine without giving any cause of offence to the other. If the desire was for a unification of the two Churches, a decision might have to be made between the two views. But for purposes of living together in peace, the two versions could have been long ago allowed to abide happily side by side without any breach in unity of doctrine between the two Churches.

The importance for us of this piece of past history is that it demonstrates that over large areas of doctrine in which the Churches have differed or may differ still, and especially where the doctrines in question are largely metaphysical and speculative, there is no need at all for the Churches to suppose that definitive agreement or synthesis is required. Generally speaking in these matters there can be no finally correct answer. In any case the laymen of the Churches cannot be expected to form judgements about such highly technical matters; nor can they be easily interested in them. Each Church has a right to retain its own traditional doctrine so long as it wants to; the various doctrines of this kind can coexist without in any way damaging the doctrinal unity of the two or more Churches. It is only when the points of doctrinal difference have practical consequences in conflicting Church disciplines or manners that it is necessary that some satisfactory working agreement be worked out for acceptance by the Churches concerned.

At the Council of Florence, besides the question of the procession of the Holy Ghost, there was discussion of the doctrine of Purgatory, leavened or unleavened bread in the Sacrament and other liturgical differences, the marriage of the clergy, and divorce, among other things. How like today it sounds. In all such cases, there is no need for 'growing together' with a view to subsequent unification. All that is needed is to make sure that the proper freedoms of each Church are preserved from unfair outside pressures, that the respective doctrines can live together reasonably without causing offence to any, and that where they cause practical conflict or complications, suitable adjustments are made.

We may consider as a case in point one of the topics now being discussed between representatives of the Church of England and the Church of Rome, the kind of degree of respect and honour to be paid to the Blessed Virgin Mary, the mother of our Lord. A few years ago a Pope decreed that belief in the Assumption of her physical body into heaven was *de fide*. There is no reason why he should not impose this belief on all Roman Catholics if his Church requires him to do so. But since the Pope then (and still) claims some kind of authority over the whole Church Militant, it became in fact an attempt to impose this doctrine as one of necessity for all Churches. It was for that reason that Archbishop Garbett of York and I of Canterbury issued a statement regretting this papal pronouncement and rejecting both the doctrine and its imposition. The point of great importance that concerns us all here is that against the Church of Rome each Church can retain its own doctrine on this matter and its own idea of how to show due reverence for the Mother of our Lord without blocking the way thereby to advance to Full Communion.

In this matter of unity in doctrine, St. Paul's words to the Galatians can be well adapted to the Churches thus. Let us bear one another's burdens, and so fulfil the law of Christ. For if any Church thinks it is something, when it is nothing, it deceives itself. But let each Church test its own work, and then its reason to boast will be in itself alone and not in its neighbour. For each Church will have to bear its own load.

Before we leave this topic, we must observe that of course it is not possible in Church relations to draw an absolute line between doctrinal interests and other interests. Many practical differences rest more on varieties of custom and temperament than of doctrine, though they are often given a doctrinal justification which cannot stand scrutiny. In the Great Schism 'the more that Eastern and Western Christendom saw of each other, the more in general they disliked what they saw'. It is a mistake to suppose that when churchmen of different Churches see a lot of each other, they necessarily grow to like what they see. The opposite may often be the case and may be so for good reasons. 'The real bar to union was that Eastern and Western Christendom felt differently about religion; and it is difficult to debate about feelings.' How true that is today of the various kinds of Catholic and Protestant Churchmen: religious feelings find different ways of expressing themselves linguistically, doctrinally, liturgically, devotionally. Thus religious language and symbol which is at home in one Church is alien in another. All these considerations point away from any kind of unification between Churches which have a strong and articulate tradition of their own. They point towards the relationship of Full Communion where each Church can preserve its own traditional doctrine and ethos and where cross fertilisation between the Churches is encouraged by a unity which is the fruit of spiritual fellowship and avoids the dangers of unification.

There is another matter which divided the Eastern and Western Churches then and divides them now. 'The discussion of differences in doctrine and in practice (at the council of Florence) was somewhat pointless when one side was determined to secure the total submission of the other'. It is safe to say that none of the particular Churches outside the Roman Communion will or should ever submit to the *Magisterium* of the Church of Rome. There is the stubborn fact with which the Church of Rome must come to terms. Meanwhile it is interesting to recall that the agreed basis of discussion at the Council of Florence was:

reference to the Holy Scriptures, the canons of the Oecumenical Councils and the works of those of the Fathers who were recognised as saints by the Universal Church.

The Eastern and Western Churches differ as to the number of Oecumenical Councils by which they are bound. The Church of England follows the ancient Fathers and Councils only so far as they are agreeable to Scripture.[1] But it is today generally acceptable in all the Churches that we must all start from the Holy Scriptures in general and from the New Testament in particular, and relying on the guidance of the Holy Spirit, given severally to all who wait upon him, must walk together in harmony of faith and good works as one company in the service of the one Lord.[2]

---

[1] See Canon A.5 (new series) and in Article 34 'Every particular or national Church hath authority to ordain, change and abolish, ceremonies or rites of the Church ordained only by man's authority, so that all things be done to edifying'.

[2] Bishop Butler, whose article in *The Tablet* was referred to earlier, wrote in it 'It should be obvious that (Full Communion) presupposes that dogmatic issues have been successfully dealt with. Throughout Church history visible unity has been the expression of a shared faith.' Later he said that 'these matters, for Catholics, include all defined dogmas of faith'. As I have tried to show in this chapter churchmen of other Churches in the Church Militant have an equal right to preserve their own definitions. Indeed, properly understood all baptised Christians are 'Catholics'.

18

Unity in Church Order

St. Paul reminds us that 'God is not a God of confusion but of peace' and bids us 'earnestly desire to prophesy and do not forbid speaking in tongues: but all things should be done decently and in order'. There must be in each particular Church of God its ministerial structure, a decent Church order, governing the preaching and teaching of the Word of God, the administration of the Sacraments of the Lord, and other sacramental acts as ordered (i.e. arranged constitutionally) by the official ministers of the Church. In the New Testament itself there is providentially only a very sketchy outline of what this structure should be. The Churches were feeling their way towards a settled order not yet discovered. When the Churches emerge from the early centuries of their existence into a settled order, it is seen that three things have become necessary parts of every Church structure and so the permanent possessions of the whole Church.

A. The New Testament is the possession of the whole Church, embodying its officially accepted records not only of the life and ministry of the Lord and Saviour Jesus Christ but also of his equipment of the Church with the essential elements of its creed, with the two Sacraments to be administered in the name of Christ and with the rudiments of its ministry. It is misleading to say simply that 'we owe the New Testament to the Church'. There were many writings, including gospels, in circulation in the Churches in early days claiming the authority of authenticity. There was controversy as to which were to be accepted as genuine. There were rival canons or authorised lists of books. A Council of the Churches ended the controversies by fixing our present canon of New Testament books for universal acceptance. Biblical scholars of the different Churches have been increasingly working together: indeed it was from this fact perhaps above all others that the oecumenical movement derived its spiritual impetus. But each Church decides entirely for itself how far it allows its official doctrine to be affected by the varying findings of the scholars as they change from time to time.

B. The Creeds were also made possessions of the whole Church by conciliar actions. They are brief summaries of the basic facts of the Church's faith, 'symbols' of the faith, put forth for the purpose of teaching the faith and protecting the faith. Each Church was and is free to use and interpret them as its doctrines may require. No Church would maintain that the three Creeds remain adequate for their original purpose for all time or for our times. But as every Church has inherited them as basic documents so each Church must respect them as such. No particular Church can add to or subtract from the Creeds or diminish the witness which they give. It was one of the charges which the Eastern Church made against the Church of Rome that it had unilaterally and without consultation presumed to alter the text of a Creed, a thing, as it maintained, which only a fully oecumenical council could do.

But on the other hand since creeds and formularies come from past ages, no Church is wise if it attempts to make its members believe in the *ipsissima verba* of ancient creeds or formularies. The Church of England requires its clergy to accept the Book of Common Prayer, which includes the Creeds, and to affirm that in their belief the doctrine therein contained is agreeable to the Word of God: and they undertake that in public prayer and administration of the Sacraments they will use the forms therein contained and none other save so far as shall be ordered by lawful authority.

That is a wise and liberal declaration of assent. It preserves a decent Church order and leaves room for a decent liberty of interpretation both to the clergy and to the laity in the ministrations which they share. There has been, as is well known, a very long period of liturgical and devotional disorder in the Church of England, during which some of the clergy failed to obey either in the letter or in the spirit this declaration of assent. They could rightly claim that there was uncertainty about the precise meaning of 'lawful authority', and they took advantage of this fact, and it was quickly found that to seek to restrain such ministers by legal proceedings did much more harm than good. A Church has to live through sad periods of disorder as best it can, until there can be a redefinition of lawful authority able to carry the co-operative obedience of the clergy and the support of the laity. Since 1945 the Church of England has laboriously but successfully redefined the meaning of lawful authority for the purposes of the Declaration of Consent. Thereby it has renewed a general sense of loyalty and obedience to the doctrine and discipline of the Church of England as set out in the Canons. At the same time it must be recognised that in times such as these all forms of obedience and authority are under strain in every Church.[1]

C. The threefold ministry is the third factor to become in early days the possession of the whole Church. Herein lay not only an essential instrument of internal security for each Church but also an essential means of communication and co-operation between the Churches of Christendom. While each Church was left free in its internal administration to control as best it could the co-operation of its bishops, priests and deacons together with some kind of consultation with and consent of the laity (which became on occasions strong and even violent pressure by them), each Church maintained this same ministerial structure. In each particular Church the bishop and the presbyters were by virtue of their ordained status the sole ministers of the Word and Sacraments and bore the sole responsibility for the government and good order of the Church, for the pastoral care of the Church community, and for its good standards of behaviour.[2]

In origin the bishop was the permanent president of the presbyters, acting with them as one of them as well as over them, as may be seen still in the fact that to this day in ordaining men to the priesthood the bishop is joined in the laying on of hands by the presbyters (otherwise priests)

---

[1] There have often been demands that the 39 Articles should be either abandoned or revised. That would be a great mistake. They are there and form one of the historic documents of the Church of England and parts of them can never become out of date. But other parts have for long been outdated. A recent report wisely recommended that the assent should be clearly assent to the historic document and not to everything in it.

[2] It is now somewhat misleading to refer to the 'threefold ministry' as a sheet anchor of the Catholic Church. The position and function of the deacons differ widely in different Churches and if the order be threefold, it must now be described as that of bishops, presbyters, and baptised laymen and lay women.

there present. But the bishop was distinguished from the presbyters by the fact that he represented the Church over which he presided in contacts with the outside world and in particular in his Church's contacts with other Churches and in the fellowship of bishops with whom he was associated in higher councils of the Church. When at the time of the Reformation some Churches became non-episcopal, they thereby created a great structural cleavage between the episcopal and non-episcopal Churches, and though they substituted parallel offices (sometimes with the title of bishop still) they were not and did not claim to be the same thing as the bishops of the original succession. This is a structural difference (carrying with it diversities also of doctrine and practice) which has to be remedied before there can be a reconciliation of Church Order between them along with the recovery of the blessings of a Full Communion in which they become equal partners in full fellowship.

In the course of history the bishops and the episcopal system in general have acquired a bad reputation among the non-episcopal Churches and with plenty to justify such a reputation. But though the office has often been misused, it is the office which by long tradition has served as a sign of the unity and continuity of the General Church. It is essentially a pastoral office. It has a flavour of apostolicity about it still. It is essentially a co-operative and a reconciling office since the bishop's oversight is designed to unite presbyters and laity with himself for the good of the family and household over which he presides in the Church of God. Beyond all doubt it has been a true means of grace to the Church at large. Now with the safeguards and challenges which the representation of clergy and laity in the government of the Churches provide, no

Church need have fears of prelacy any more than of over-bearing influence from ministers or laity, and no Church need lack the power to keep the three Orders of bishops, presbyters and laity in a due proportion of constructive power and spiritual leadership. All other Churches are watching the Church of Rome with keen interest, with some anxiety and with a profound sympathy for it in its travails and with united prayer for a happy issue from them as it addresses itself to the tasks of reformation to which it has become pledged through the inspiration of Pope John XXIII and the labours of Vatican II, a great part of which is concerned with the reordering of the relationships of bishops, priests and laity to one another and with the relation of the whole Church of Rome itself to its papacy in a form which is scriptural, tolerable and fraternal. As we shall see the way to Full Communion between the Churches of the General Church requires a general acceptance of the episcopal structure. The real obstacle to agreement in the Church is to be found not so much in episcopacy as in the question of priesthood in relation to Church Order.

19

Priesthood and Sacrifice

By striking across the open moors, we can avoid many miles of tedious and toilsome main roads, carrying the centuries-old traffic of sacerdotal and presbyteral controversy, main roads which nowadays only theologians care to travel on foot and which lay people are glad to cover by fast coach or private car, if at all.

We begin with the word 'priest' and must observe that nowhere in the New Testament is the presbyter or bishop or other officer of the New Testament Churches called a priest. For that there must be a reason, and the reason is quite clear. The religious system of the Jews had at its heart and centre the worship of the Temple with its elaborate system of priesthood and the offering of animal and other sacrifices, a system hallowed by the ages and part of the Mosaic Law of their forefathers, details of which are preserved for us in the pages of the Old Testament. In the same world existed the Greek and Roman traditions of worship with their systems of priests, priestesses and sacrifices. No doubt the Christian Church avoided calling any of its officers priests in the first place in order to avoid calling up the alien ideas of Jewish or pagan priesthood.

St. Peter in his first epistle calls the Church 'a chosen race, a royal priesthood, a holy nation, God's own people' but he refers to the officers of the Christians of Asia Minor to whom he wrote as presbyters and calls himself a fellow presbyter with them. There are in the New Testament many words or phrases deeply coloured by the priestly and sacrificial language of the Old Testament. It would be astonishing if Jewish Christians like St. Paul and St. Peter did not sometimes use the familiar words and ideas of the religion in which they were nurtured, as they spoke of Christ and his sacrifice for the world and his priestly work for mankind. So still on Easter Day in the Easter Anthems we sing: 'Christ our passover is sacrificed for us: therefore let us keep the feast'. In the Proper Preface for that day we say: 'for he is the very Paschal Lamb which was offered for us' and in the Gloria we say 'O Lord God, Lamb of God, Son of the Father'. Our traditional language speaks in prayers and hymns of Christ as Priest and Victim on the Cross. It would be unreasonable to expect the Churches to abandon the application to Christ our Redeemer of ideas and language thus drawn from Old Testament sources. Our Lord himself told us that salvation is from the Jews. But we must never forget that as we are clearly told in the New Testament, Christ changed the old ideas of priesthood by a total fulfilment of them which transmuted them to a higher level of spiritual truth.

The evidence of the revolutionary change thus made is to be found recorded most clearly in the story of the council held in Jerusalem at the request of the Church in Antioch, as recorded in the Acts of the Apostles.[1] Paul and Barnabas, back at Antioch from a great missionary expedition, declared to the Church there all that God had done with them, showing how he had 'opened a door of faith to the Gentiles'. Some time later Christians from Judaea came to Antioch and taught that Gentiles could not be saved unless they were circumcised according to the custom of Moses. This was evidently a direct challenge to all that Paul and Barnabas had been teaching to Gentiles.

[1] Acts of the Apostles, ch. 15.

The Church of Antioch sent Paul and Barnabas and others to put the problem before the Jerusalem Church, and 'they were welcomed by the Church and the apostles and presbyters'. It may be noted both that the laity took part in the proceedings and that of the original apostles only Peter is named as having been present, while James the brother of the Lord and president of the Jerusalem Church was in the chair. It was a hearing by the local Church in Jerusalem on an important question concerning inherited Jewish law. Peter and Paul were both important witnesses and both were to be heard in the debate. At its close James summed up and gave it as his judgement that the Gentile Christians should not be troubled with the law of Moses: it was a law meant only for Jews, and if Jewish Christians wanted to honour it they could hear Moses read every Sabbath in the synagogues. The whole Jerusalem Church then sent leading members of the community with a letter addressed to 'the brethren who are of the Gentiles in Antioch and Syria and Cilicia' saying 'It has seemed good to the Holy Spirit and to us to lay upon you no greater burden than these necessary things'. The necessary things were to refrain from idolatry, unchastity, 'blood and what is strangled': for the rest the Mosaic Law could be forgotten. Thus Gentiles for all time were liberated from all the concepts and practices of priesthood and sacrifice as contained in the law of Moses as part of the old covenant between God and his people.

The doctrinal implications of this revolutionary change are indicated by the unknown author of the Epistle to the Hebrews, writing (it would seem) to exhort discouraged Jewish converts not to look back to the Judaism they had abandoned but to persevere in their Christian faith. He assured them that Christ had summed up in his own person and in his own sacrifice all that priesthood and sacrifice had meant under the Mosaic Law, and had so become the saviour and liberator, the eternal High Priest, for Christians and indeed for all mankind.

Thus:

> By the which will we are sanctified, through the offering of the body of Jesus Christ once for all. And every priest standeth daily ministering, and offering oftentimes the same sacrifices, which can never take away sins. But this man after he had offered one sacrifice for sins for ever, sat down on the right hand of God . . . For by a single offering he hath perfected for ever those that are sanctified.

or again:

> Since then we have a great high priest who has passed through the heavens, Jesus the Son of God, let us hold fast our confession. For we have not a high priest who is unable to sympathise with our weaknesses, but one who in every respect has been tempted as we are, yet without sinning. Let us then with confidence draw near to the throne of grace, that we may receive mercy and find grace to help in time of need.

or yet again:

> By a single offering (of himself) he has perfected for all time those who are sanctified . . . Therefore, brethren, since we have confidence to enter the sanctuary by the blood of Jesus, by the new and living way which he opened for us . . . through his flesh, and since we have a great priest over the house of God, let us draw near with a true heart in full assurance of faith, with our hearts sprinkled clean from all evil conscience and our bodies washed with pure water. Let us hold fast the confession of our hope without wavering, for he who promised is faithful.

It may then be said with confidence that in the New Testament itself the point from which all the Churches start, all the earthly possibilities of priesthood and sacrifice are fulfilled by Christ in his incarnation, that for the ministers of his Church the right name is presbyter rather than priest, and the right description of the Church's sacrifices is the sacrifice of obedience together with the sacrifice of praise and thanksgiving.

Through many centuries theologians have endeavoured very properly to elaborate this original New Testament theology, to illuminate it, to expand it and (must one not say?) also and often dangerously to emotionalise it both by bringing back into it much of the flavour of Old Testament priesthood and sacrifice and by putting into the liturgies of the Church the idea of a priest who has something that he must 'offer' by virtue of his priesthood. At the Reformation the Reformed Churches rejected much of this elaboration of patristic and mediaeval thought on priesthood and sacrifice. The Church of England is firmly on the side of this reformed doctrine.

The grand conclusion to which we can now thankfully and faithfully come is even when two Churches hold different and even opposed views on the working out of ideas of priesthood and sacrifice, yet they can live trustfully together on the sure foundation provided by the New Testament teaching,[1] and if they have reasonably reconciled and co-ordinated their methods of ministerial administration, can proceed to Full Communion in full enjoyment of the way of truth, unity of spirit and righteousness of life.

[1] It must be emphasised once again that while St. Peter in his first epistle described the Church as being (amongst other things) a royal and a holy priesthood, he conspicuously did not describe either himself, an apostle, or those whom he hailed as fellow presbyters as 'priests'. This point is often overlooked by those who may be described as sacerdotalists. Since there is always some danger involved in attributing to offices or things the essentially personal quality of holiness, we may note that in his epistle St. Peter also emphasises the personal nature of holiness. 'The One who called you is holy; like him, be holy in all your behaviour, because Scripture says "You shall be holy, for I am holy".'

20

Authority in the Churches

EVERY churchman ought to have some understanding of the way in which the principle of authority operates in the General Church. Each of the Churches will have its own particular structural pattern of authority in action; but there is necessarily, since every Church is a Church of Christ, a strong resemblance between all their structural patterns even if there are also strong differences. With the pattern of the Church of England as the one I know best, I try to give an idea of the general pattern, and begin, as we always must from principles found in the New Testament.

Jesus Christ seemed to take it for granted in all his teaching, that each one of his followers, each Christian, is responsible in his own person in all things to God and is thus his own final authority over himself. St. Paul states this principle thus to the Corinthians—'the spiritual man judges all things, but is himself to be judged by no one', and by the spiritual man he means one baptised into the fellowship of the Church. It is on this principle that the right to freedom of conscience rests not only for Christians but for men in general. There are obviously limitations of his freedom in civic life. In the life of the Church it is to be expected that the Christian in exercising his rights to freedom of conscience will at the same time conscientiously respect the honour which he owes to the community of his Church and to God, using such means as are available to him for the training of his conscience, especially by prayer and intelligent study, so that he may come to right and wise judgements, ever sensitive to what he knows or should know of the good and acceptable and perfect will of God, and (it is to be hoped) ever sensitive to recognise the kind of mistakes of judgement to which he is specially liable through the tendencies or weaknesses of his own mental and moral temperament.

But there is the authority of the Church which the individual Christian is bound to respect. It is indeed part of the duty laid on him by Christ to love his neighbour as himself. But all forms of authority inside or outside the Church are prone to entertain or to provoke idolatries and selfishnesses of one kind and another. In any society things will go wrong unless there is an intelligent and sensitive and domestic understanding holding together in a reasonable harmony all holders of authority whether of high or low degree, and resulting in a generous and active spirit of co-operation. This is something of what is meant by the phrase now much used of Co-responsibility in the Church.[1] It serves to emphasise that churchmen, realising the perils of disharmony, need constantly and earnestly to pray for themselves and for their fellow churchmen of all Churches the collect for Whit Sunday that God will 'grant us by the same Spirit to have a right judgement in all things'.

In the traditional structure of the Church, the congregations (which have a degree of authority of their own which must not be neglected) are gathered together for necessary purposes of pastoral administration into dioceses. At the head of each diocese is its bishop, the pastoral and administrative head of his family—charged with the duty of being

[1] Not to be confused with another word, collegiality. The word refers properly to the supposed authority of all bishops in the Catholic Church as members of a College of Bishops. The word should properly refer, as I think, to the College of Bishops, presbyters and laity in each diocese.

a chief pastor and not in any sense a prelate. 'Be to the flock of Christ a shepherd not a wolf' says the Ordinal at the consecration of a bishop, echoing words of Christ himself: 'Hold up the weak, heal the sick, bind up the broken, bring again the outcasts, seek the lost'. This of course he can only begin to do if all the people in his diocese are doing it with him. And then the Ordinal goes on to say a word about the use of his authority: 'Be so merciful, that you be not too remiss: so minister discipline, that you forget not mercy'—the permanent dilemma of all who hold any kind of authority whoever they may be.

Thus the bishop is the focus of unity in each diocese. An early Father, Cyprian of Carthage, regarding Peter as the first bishop and Father (Pope) of the Christian Church, considered that all subsequent bishops were of equal rank and honour with him, and each bishop was his own Pope in his own diocese. There is truth in that, but it was soon realised as the Church expanded that dioceses could not stand alone in a hostile world, but must be associated together in wider groupings of dioceses. We should be unwise to follow Cyprian into thinking that the General Church ought to be governed by a General Council of the whole body of bishops from every part of the Church, an idea which is at the root of the principle of collegiality, much talked about since Vatican II. The diocesan bishops, while having a special authority in their own dioceses as being the focus of their united life, have traditionally been grouped in national or regional Churches, such as the Churches of Jerusalem, Alexandria, Antioch and Rome.[1]

[1] I take these representative names from Article 19 which also says that all these Churches have erred not only in their living and manner of ceremonies, but also in matters of faith. How true, not only of these Churches but of the Church of England and every other Church as well. But so wisely Article 20 goes on to say that every Church has power to decree rites or ceremonies and authority in controversies of faith.

It should be noted here that not all national or regional Churches are episcopal with bishops and dioceses. Thus in Great Britain the Church of Scotland is a presbyterian Church. Nor is it to be supposed now that in any one nation or region there will be only one Church. There are many regional Churches living side by side in all countries, some with bishops presiding over dioceses, others with moderators or superintendents presiding over districts or other areas of jurisdiction and pastoral care.

Each national or regional Church has the problem of authority within its own boundaries and within those boundaries is autonomous, governing and disciplining itself with its own authority as a Church of Christ within the General Church. It has, of course, relations with the other Churches within the same nation or region and with yet wider families of Churches. We shall consider those relationships under the general heading of intercommunion. Here we are doing no more than describing the general pattern of authority to be found in all Churches. There are the chief officers, bishops or others, who exercise the general control or oversight and as such have their own distinctive degree of authority. With or under them are two classes of churchmen, those ordained to the Ministry of the Word and Sacraments and those by baptism and episcopal confirmation (or it may be by some equivalent in non-episcopal Churches) admitted to the responsibilities of lay membership.

We have said enough of the authority of the bishops. The authority of the ordained minister is a functional authority, the authority which naturally adheres to the functions which he is ordained and commissioned to discharge on behalf of the Church. He has a pastoral function, a preaching and teaching function, in some degree a prophetic function. He has a presbyteral function which certainly includes contributing the wisdom and stability of judgement and impartial devotion that goes with maturity of experience and age. He has a priestly function in that he is entrusted with that kind of service and ministry which flows from his Church's understanding of priesthood in the New Testament. There has from the earliest days been dispute, often bitter, as to what a priest is appointed or enabled to do by his ordination. It may be enough to say that it is never easy and may perhaps be altogether unnecessary to distinguish between what a minister does as pastor and what he does as priest, and that the best thing to do is to say that what he does whether as pastor or as priest in the appointed sacraments of the Church is sufficiently comprehended without further definition in the title 'presbyter' as it is in the first epistle of St. Peter.[1]

The layman of course has his authority too which is at long last being recognised formally and officially in the constitutional systems of the Church of England and, I believe, of the Church of Rome. But here there is a point of great importance not fully appreciated. If the laity are brought by one way or another into the counsels of the Church, that must mean that they must be consulted in doctrinal matters as well as in the practical side of the Church's life and it may at once be said that the laity cannot have the same authority in matters of doctrine as that which belongs to the ordained clergy. The matter is far from simple. Perhaps we should distinguish broadly between the technical aspects of doctrine and the general

[1] Cf. Richard Hooker: 'whether we call it a priesthood, a presbytership, or a Ministry it skilleth not: although in truth the word *Presbyter* doth seem more fit, and in propriety of speech more agreeable than *Priest* with the drift of the whole Gospel of Jesus Christ.'

aspects of doctrine. It will be only some of the clergy who are competent judges in the technical aspects of doctrine, in the general aspects there will not be much to choose between intelligent clergymen and intelligent laymen and both alike will be readier to appreciate the moral aspects than the technical aspects of matters under discussion. Moreover both alike need some measure of protection against the ideas of those who are thinking in terms no longer relevant or who are propagandists for a system of fixed ideas. What is certain is that if the laity are to play their proper part in the life and mission of the Church, they must be kept in living touch (as they have not been in the past) with the essentials of New Testament doctrine and must be enabled to discriminate wisely, when required to form judgements on questions of current theological importance. Many of the clergy will have the same needs as the laity: but if they set out to make themselves competent to meet the needs of the laity in these respects, they will thereby train themselves to be wise and progressive students of doctrine after a new pattern to the great benefit of the whole Church. Clergy and laity will become for the first time partners along with their bishops in doctrinal alertness as well as in evangelistic zeal, and in both after the examples set in the New Testament rather than after the speculative teachings of Fathers and Councils.

There are of course those with other degrees of authority, official or unofficial, on boards or committees or groups, according to their respective skills and abilities. In the governing bodies of the Church all alike, clergy and laity, whether reactionary or reforming in spirit, will have to take their part through representatives, and no system of representation is ever altogether satisfactory. It is thus that the *consensus fidelium* which is accepted as the final authority in every Church finds its expression. But there is no one able to say with absolute authority who are the *fideles* in the Church and no one to say how successfully their *consensus* has been ascertained.[1] Security must always depend upon the degree in which all who share in the Church's authority observe the counsel of St. James:

> Where jealousy and selfish ambition exist, there will be disorder and every vile practice. But the wisdom from above is first pure, then peaceable, gentle, open to reason, full of mercy and good fruits, without uncertainty or insincerity. And the harvest of righteousness is sown in peace by those who make peace.

[1] A Roman Catholic authority has said to me in a private letter: 'I agree that this . . . would tend to suggest that the *census* (*sic*) *fidelium* is a regulative idea rather than a concrete principle. But Roman Catholics would say that in the end, and at certain critical moments, the Episcopate and/or the Papacy gives expression to the *census fidelium*, as e.g. at the first Council of Nicaea.'

21

Unity in Intercommunion

GREAT care is needed in the use of this word. It is very commonly supposed to refer in some way to the Holy Communion: but that is not so. The word 'communion' (or in the Greek *koinonia*) is a general word for a having-in-common, or fellowship. It is the Church as a separate society which is a fellowship and by intercommunion is meant all those activities which can take place between Churches in which members of different Churches are able to take part freely. For participation in such activities members of a Church ought to have the authority or the general good will of the Church to which they belong whether formally expressed or not. But when formal ministerial and sacramental acts are involved authority more precise than this is required. Short of such acts, activities of intercommunion between clergy and congregations may grow up spontaneously from the promptings of Christian fellowship or under the encouragement and impetus of some general movement like the oecumenical movement. In the development of this spirit of unity and Christian fellowship the British Council of Churches and the World Council of Churches, both of which owed so much to Archbishop William Temple, have played a great part: and in their conferences and assemblies the Churches became accustomed not only to thinking together but to praying together, to oecumenical services and to official sharing in one another's services, whether on a great scale or in smaller gatherings equally impressive

and fruitful. This movement of Intercommunion in joint
Church activities has been multiplying daily, and especially since the Church of Rome, which till recently held
aloof, has come to take a full part with the rest of us. But
there is a need for some restraints. This kind of impetus
for unity may easily lead to some disorders or unwise
blurring of real differences. Some may want to go beyond
what their Churches have approved so that liberty may
look too much like licence. Others may come to think that
no differences matter and that acting together is all. And
in the excellence and excitement of this progress in Unity
of Spirit, there is some danger that adjustments of doctrine
may be made or demanded without sufficiently precise
thought and examination. At one time there was a separate organisation, called Faith and Order, closely associated with the World Council of Churches but independent
of it, on which men of scholarly knowledge and gifts from
the Churches considered and advised on doctrinal subjects. I greatly regretted it when the World Council
abolished its independence and took it over as one of its
own departments, thereby depriving the essential subjects
of Faith and Order of some of the particular respect due
to them and exposing them too much to the enthusiasms
of those who are impatient of structural or doctrinal
restraints. However that may be, we can rejoice that this
great movement of Intercommunion has so marvellously
moved: nor is it to belittle it to say that there is some
danger in the Lund Dictum that everything which the
Churches *can* do together they *should* do together. It is
certainly not true to say of Christian families living as
neighbours that they should aim at doing together everything that can be done together. No one can measure
the value of those things which a family does in its own

separate family life, thereby expressing and developing
their bonds of domestic affection and the characteristic
loyalties and graces of their unity as a family. The doing of
very much by the Churches together must not be allowed
to weaken the graciousness of what each Church does
separately, thereby helping it effectively to make its own
characteristic contribution to the General Church. There
is a danger in overdoing the doing together, especially
when it involves not only world-scale councils but ever
increasing measures of world organisation and the planning of grandiose operations to produce (as the recent
Lambeth Conference suggested) 'An oecumenical forum
on the widest possible scale' so that 'a genuinely universal
council may once more speak for all Christians'.[1]

I have noted above that the activities of Intercommunion must stop short at a certain point. Joint action in
the official ministerial and sacramental services of a
Church need the express authority of the Churches concerned and comes to be considered in connection with the
more intimate relationship between Churches known as
Full Communion which covers the whole range of inter-
Church fellowship activities ministerial and sacramental.
Naturally as Churches have become more and more close
to each other in activities of Intercommunion, the desire
for Full Communion has become more and more felt and
has become more insistent, but not always according to
knowledge. It was supposed by some that the Holy
Communion, the chief sacramental act of the General
Church, had been given in some way to the General
Church as such and therefore ought to be accessible in

---

[1] It must always be a disaster when top level organisation of a Church or
of the Church destroys its essentially domestic character and its character
as basically a *consensus fidelium*.

every Church to all communicants of *any* Church. But in truth the Apostles gave the Holy Communion and everything else they had to give to the particular Churches, and each Church from the first bore its own responsibility for the administration of the Sacraments as for its preaching of the Word of God. This structure of Church Order and Doctrine is to be respected with utter faithfulness; and no one Church must presume to judge its fellows in their manner of doing it lightly or wantonly. This line between Intercommunion and Full Communion is an absolute line, controlled in each Church by its own authority. There is a lurking danger in the phrase 'our unhappy divisions'. Hostile divisions between Churches, showing themselves in contests of power and prestige and doctrinal supremacy have worked untold damage to the General Church, to the souls of men and to their understandings of the kingdom of God. But not all divisions have been of this sort. Some are due to natural causes, some to cultural and domestic causes, many to what may be called non-theological causes but are not therefore without value or validity. When all Churches come to be in Full Communion with each other as they should, there will remain, one may hope, certain divisions, friendly and fruitful, between the autonomous Churches, with separate identities and integrities still, yet sacramentally made one.

4

22

Unity in Full Communion

THE One General Church always has been and always will be an undivided Church insomuch as it is the society of baptised members of the Body of Christ living in the world in the faith of Christ as recorded in the New Testament and renewed in faithful disciples by the Holy Spirit in each succeeding age. As we have seen it is made visible through the life and witness of particular autonomous Churches and especially through the activities of Intercommunion in which they share together in bearing witness to the Christian Faith. But as we have also seen each Church has its own structure of Faith and Order, and if two or more autonomous Churches are to be in Full Communion without losing their separate identities, there must be a satisfactory adjustment of their respective structures of Faith and Order, of doctrine and of ministry and administration. Part of this adjustment demands a full fellowship between the Churches concerned in their celebration and administration of the sacrament of the Holy Communion: but that is not in itself enough. There must be such a trust and so clear an agreement in faith between the Churches concerned that they no longer wish to question or criticise their respective ways of doing things, freely accepting one another as they are with all the proper freedoms that belong to an autonomous Church of Christ in the wider fellowship of the General Church.

We have already seen something of what should be meant by the proper freedoms to be retained by each Church in matters of doctrine. All alike accept the authority of the New Testament as their starting point, providing them with the essentials of the Christian Gospel and of Church life, devotion and service: but within that generous unity of faith, each Church may rightly hold its own tradition of the doctrinal, liturgical, devotional, cultural and ethical application of them to its own particular circumstances and requirements: though in so doing it must keep carefully in sympathetic touch with other Churches, so that diversities of operations may not become causes of offence. Thus at this time it is opportune to observe that each Church is free to use its own judgement on such matters as women priests or celibacy or the use of contraceptives since none of these matters can be shown to be governed by any binding New Testament or theological principle. The recent discussions between the Church of England and the Methodist Church have shown that so far as general doctrinal matters are concerned there is nothing to hinder immediate advance to Full Communion. There is agreement in essentials and no further precise agreements are to be regarded as essential.

The same Anglican/Methodist discussions have greatly clarified the position as to inter-Church adjustments in ministerial structure required for Full Communion. It was proposed by the Commission concerned with this matter that the Methodist Church should 'take episcopacy into its system' by appointing ministers to be made bishops of the Methodist Church and securing their due consecration as bishops in the General Church of God.[1] Thus the

[1] The Commission proposed that they should be consecrated by bishops of the Church of England: but this is in no way a necessity and might cause misunderstanding. A leading Methodist minister has suggested to me that the Church of South India should be asked to provide for the Service of Consecration in which case some of their bishops who were formerly ministers of the Methodist Church in South India could be among the consecrators along with some who were formerly Anglican ministers.

deepest structural division would disappear: and episcopacy would have been accepted on the good and secure foundation that it has been from very early times the continuous sign of the unity and continuity of Churches within the General Church. But there would still remain the need to reconcile for a co-operative ministry in the new relationship existing Anglican and Methodist ministers who have all been already ordained to the ministry of the Word and Sacraments of the Church of God in their respective Churches, Anglicans *with* and Methodists *without* episcopal ordination. The suggestion made in the Commission's report that there should be in the Service of Reconciliation a kind of prayer and laying on of hands sufficient to secure episcopal ordination *'if that is what is needed'* could not be regarded as an acceptable one since it denies or casts doubts upon the sufficiency of the ordination into the ministry of the Church of God already received by the Methodist ministers coming to be reconciled. If this suggestion is withdrawn, then (as the Commission also mentions as a possibility) each Church would accept the ministers of the other Church for what they profess themselves to be by their existing ordination, and would then by prayer[1] and the laying on of hands, commission them to exercise the functions of a presbyter in its own Churches and for its own congregations. Thus the structural barrier in the administration of the Holy Communion affecting Methodist ministers ordained before the time of Methodist bishops would be overcome and the way to Full Communion would be immediately made open.

This way of reconciling existing ministers ordained

---

[1] It is essential that the prayer should be identical for all its users, asking God to bestow on all the ministers to be reconciled every spiritual grace, authority and blessing for their ministry in Full Communion. Thus it is clear that God alone does the reconciling.

some with, some without episcopal ordination, in Churches of different traditions has already been adopted by Anglican, Methodist and other Churches of Ceylon which are to become a United Church, and has received the approval and blessing of the Lambeth Conferences of 1958 and 1968. Moreover if the disruptive suggestion of prayers differing in wording and in significance is withdrawn, it becomes reasonable to hope that in due course the Church of Scotland and other Presbyterian Churches will be able to consider acceptance of episcopacy interpreted as no more but no less than a sign of the unity and continuity of the Church of God as a step to the blessings of Full Communion with the Episcopal Churches in the one Church of God. As regards the Church of Rome, there is already a belief growing in that Church that it should recognise Anglican Orders as of equal standing with those of the Orthodox Communion. The differences of doctrine between the Church of England and the Church of Rome are under consideration already by representatives of the two Churches. If they hope to grow together in these discussions to a general unanimity of doctrine, they will certainly fail. But if they are content to discover how, without disloyalty to the essential doctrines of the Church, the two Churches can live together, each preserving its own traditions as legitimate, but not exclusive, derivations from the faith once delivered to the Apostles, they should quickly reach sufficient agreement for the purposes of Full Communion. The obstacle here is of another kind. Hitherto the Church of Rome has demanded from the Orthodox Communion and the Anglican Communion alike (and from all other Churches) total submission. It is to be hoped that in these days of more Christian understanding of the evidence they will accept the fact that they cannot reasonably expect submission from the other Churches and ought no longer to demand it and indeed can no longer advance the old arguments by which they used to justify their claims. It is hard indeed for an imperialist Church to accept the lowlier position of an autonomous Church, among other autonomous Churches, a Church of immense size and significance but still no more than a Church among its fellow Churches in the General Church of God. But it is no longer impossible to believe that in one way or another this understanding of itself will come about. Nor need we wait for the relationship to be formally or openly or explicitly adopted. Once it is recognised that in special needs or circumstances, Anglicans may receive communion in the Church of Rome or Roman Catholics in Anglican Churches then time may be trusted to deal with the problem of working a way to official Full Communion. In our pursuit of a General Church united throughout its range in the bonds of Universal Full Communion, we can be well content with 'here a little and there a little' so long as all is in the right direction and in the Spirit of a unity such as God wills.[1]

[1] In an article in *The Tablet* of 7th March, 1970 Bishop B. C. Butler has taken a bold initiative in introducing (for the first time so far as I know) into the thinking of Roman Catholic theologians the *idea* of Full Communion between the Church of Rome and other Churches.

23

Ruling a Church

EACH Church has, to guide it in its task of ruling itself, in addition to the New Testament, the lessons by way of warning and of inspiration of its own past and of General Church history, the current wisdoms and unwisdoms of its fellow Churches, its own national and regional gifts of character, insight and enterprise—and above all the presence of the Holy Spirit with all its members in their personal and corporate decisions.

A society or community may be ruled by dictation from the top, by pressures from the rank and file, or by a co-operative consensus. Churches have been ruled in all these methods, and the Church of England has knowledge of them all. The spiritual essence of the Reformation settlement under Queen Elizabeth I was a co-operative search for a new synthesis of Catholic and Evangelical inheritances from the New Testament. The co-operation then and since has very often given way to conflict, bitter conflict, between ultra-catholic ideas relying on some kind of infallible Church and ultra-evangelical ideas resting on some kind of infallible Bible. The last century saw the break-up of the idea of an infallible Bible: this century is witnessing the break-up of the idea of an infallible Church. There is much to encourage us to believe that in the reign of Queen Elizabeth II the Church of England is recovering with other Churches the spirit and rule of a new co-operative search for a new synthesis based on a common catholic evangel derived from the New Testament and

enriched both by the splendours and by the tragedies of
past Church history.

The first necessity for any civilised society is the rule of
Law and Order, just as its breakdown is a warning of
approaching anarchy. I have found in my own experience
of the Church Militant the first evidence of a return from
conflict to consensus in the fact that the Church of
England has now completed revision of its Canon Law.
Canon Law is a formal statement of the basic principles
on which the government of the Church rests and of the
rules in its direction and administration which its clergymen are to obey. The existing rules governing the clergy
of the Church of England had been made in 1603 and
never since revised. They were utterly out of date and
useless: but still each minister at his ordination promised
to pay 'true and canonical obedience' to his bishop 'in all
things lawful and honest', when no real meaning could be
given to the word 'canonical' while to those whose duty it
was to administer the Oath of Canonical Obedience it
was a constant spiritual scandal. There was inevitably
uncertainty and abuse of such a situation. The work of
revision begun in 1947 and carried on through endless
discussion has been completed and the new code published
in the year 1969. It has given to the Church of England a
workable set of rules: the working out of them has brought
together in discussion and understanding people of diverse
and diverging schools of thought: above all it has restored
to the clergy of the Church of England the vitally necessary sense that the Church of England has its own authority and that it is the first duty of its priests and deacons to
be loyal to that authority. It is of course never to be forgotten that the rules are shaped in obedience to the
doctrine of the Church; and the first canons of the new

code point every member of the Church of England to the New Testament, to the Thirty-nine Articles, to the Book of Common Prayer and to the Ordinal for the doctrine of the Church of England.

A society must also have means of enforcing obedience upon its members. The old system of ecclesiastical courts in the Church of England had long ago broken down. Along with the revision of Canon Law has gone a revision of the ecclesiastical courts with a jurisdiction accepted by clergy and laity alike. It was natural that the clergy who were the people liable to be brought before the ecclesiastical courts for misdemeanours, taught by history, should try to secure all proper safeguards to protect themselves from any kind of unjust treatment. As a result the new system is extremely complicated and laborious in its working, far more so than should be the case in a Christian brotherhood: but the important thing is that it is there and so bears its witness to the fact that Canon Law is there to be obeyed. But the real strength of Canon Law lies in the fact that the bishop can appeal to the loyalty of his priests and deacons to obey in the letter and in the spirit this code of rules in accordance with their oath of canonical obedience. Administration thus rests as all administration always ought to rest on truth and wise personal discretion between ruler and ruled. But even this will not suffice unless the code of rules is kept up to date; and very properly there is now a permanent body of the Church Assembly[1] charged with the duty of keeping the code of rules up to date and under constant revision.

But the revision of Canon Law has led to a far greater

[1] I have left this title as it was when I wrote; it has since been changed and the Church Assembly is now the General Synod of the Church of England. No one can say yet what difference the change will make.

reform in the system of governing the Church of England. The revision fell to be made according to precedent by the two Convocations of Canterbury and York, entirely clerical bodies. Some of the House of Laity claimed that they should have a share in the revision process, since while only the clergy had to obey the Canons, the laity lived and possibly suffered under what the clergy were appointed to do. To give the laity an equal share with the clergy in the revision of Canon Law would require a great constitutional change, and a committee under the then Dean of Christ Church, Oxford was set up to consider the constitutional issue. Meanwhile it was agreed that every proposal which was provisionally adopted by the Convocations for inclusion in the new code of Canons should be submitted for comment to the House of Laity. This meant a most cumbersome and tedious procedure in which the two Houses of Bishops, the two Houses of Clergy and the House of Laity had to consider and vote on every proposal and every amendment to every proposal before it could be finally adopted. Patience and grace in the end triumphed and the work was done. But while this was in progress, the steps towards the constitutional change were also in progress. It was slow and difficult also, truth to tell largely because some of the clergy were very unwilling to see the House of Laity put on an equality with themselves in the consideration of doctrinal matters. This itself was of course a question involving doctrine. Several times the clerical interest all but carried the day: but in the end the true doctrine triumphed that in the Church of God all must have a voice in the service of God, and the laity must have a voice of equal responsibility with the clergy. The new General Synod of the Church of England will consist as the Church Assembly consisted of the Houses of

Bishops, Clergy and Laity, but the Houses of Clergy and Laity will have equal powers in all matters which come before the General Synod, whether concerned with temporalities or with spiritualities. The Convocations will continue as before with their special interests and their special training, but with no more power of veto over what the General Synod may decide than the House of Laity has.

So the Church of England is governed and ruled by three representative bodies, the Bench of Bishops, the elected representatives of the clergy and the elected representatives of the laity. There are always possible difficulties where the people are governed through elected representatives. There are clearly special difficulties where one group of representatives, the clerical group, have had a special theological training in the doctrine and discipline of the Church of England which the other group of representatives, the lay group, lacks. To meet these difficulties there are two very important weapons. First Synodical Government itself underlines the fact that the basic ideas of Church doctrine must always be simple in principle, but are always liable to be obscured, as all Church history shows, by theological controversy and clerical professional self-interest. Laymen not infrequently have a wiser judgement in ecclesiastical matters than some of the clergy. It is right therefore that the two Houses should be forced to explain themselves to each other and so to arrive at a consensus and conclusion. And this emphasises the fact that the clergy in their parishes and elsewhere should be specially careful not to load their teaching with acquired prejudices or with speculative fancies but to teach intelligently that which gives liberal strength to the doctrine and discipline of the Church of

England. Thus the Church will be governed by Houses of well informed and loyal hearted clerical and lay representatives, each sturdily exercising his own wise discretion.

And the second all important weapon is to be found in the Bench of Bishops. They oversee the clergy and laity of their dioceses and of the Church. They are Father in God to both alike. They have sympathy with both and by office and by grace can and should interpret each to the other, reconcile where reconciliation is needed and lift both above the dust and weariness of pedestrian faith. It has been my experience that on the whole where in the Church Assembly clergy are wanting to go one way and laity the other, the bishops more often than not side with the laity—a warning how easy it is for members of a profession to be led astray by sincere professional zeal. In all honesty I must add that recently I have observed some signs of the Bench of Bishops corporately failing in its duty of dispassionate overseeing, and itself taking a professional clerical view and seeking to press it even against the views of substantial numbers of the clergy and the laity. Individual bishops may very properly hold and give expression to their own views even if, as has often been the case in the past, they may veer towards the ultra-catholic or the ultra-evangelical or the ultra-individualist: but it is a very different matter when the Bench of Bishops itself seems to be taking a corporate line of its own without due consideration of the feelings and judgements of clergy or laity in the parishes. And, one must add, it is not always possible to discover, or wise to try to discover, what the clergy and laity in the dioceses and parishes are thinking on complicated doctrinal issues by referring such matters to the dioceses to be voted on in Diocesan or Ruridecanal

Synods unless the issues have been already reduced to a number of clear and decisive questions in which a plain 'Yes' or 'No' can be fairly asked for.

Under any system of Church government it is always difficult to keep the contribution due from bishops, clergy and laity, from the whole people of God in an autonomous Church, in a right and godly proportion and so secure in its governing actions a wise and proper combination of the elements required for a wholesome *consensus fidelium* in the life of the Church. We may be humbly thankful that we have a system at least as good as that of any other Church by which clergy and laity together may co-operate in mutual trust in the ruling of the Church and in the pursuit of a Christian life. It is with deep interest and sympathy that we should observe the Church of Rome as it sets out to reform its system of government and in doing so is encountering some of the same storms and tempests that have for long beset the Church of England. All Churches have to steer their course without the possibility any longer of trusting to any kind of infallibility in Bible or in Church. Nor is it sensible for any Church to say, as has recently been said, that 'the service of the Church to the world is and must be discharged mainly by the laity' unless in the ruling of the Church a well-informed laity takes its proper share along with a well-informed clergy under a wise episcopate.

24

Unity in the Holy Communion

THE General Church derived from Jesus Christ two particular sacraments, Baptism and the Holy Communion.
The New Testament reference for the one is 'Go therefore
and make disciples of all nations, baptising them in the
name of the Father and of the Son and of the Holy Spirit';
for the other 'Do this in remembrance of me'. Each of
them consists of an action accompanied with words identi-
fying the action. Each Church within the General Church
has received those two sacraments and is directly responsible for administering them carefully and conscientiously.[1]

By baptism persons are admitted and received by the
agency of some particular Church into the General
Church. This can be so because there is general agreement
throughout all the Churches as to what constitutes baptism—the use of water and the trinitarian formula: and
it is now generally agreed that a person once baptised into
Christ by one Church cannot be baptised a second time
by another Church. That having been said, each Church
remains responsible to Christ for the conditions governing
its administration of this sacrament and also for the doctrinal interpretation it officially gives of its meaning, provided only that the sacramental act is accepted as a new
birth into 'the congregation of Christ's flock'. Churches
may differ and do differ as to any further meanings to be

[1] It is salutary to recall that the only record in the New Testament of the
discharge of this responsibility by a Church shows it as neither careful nor
conscientious (1 Cor. 11).

read into the Sacrament. They have every right to do so. St. Peter and St. Paul in their epistles give very different interpretations of the meaning of baptism.

The Holy Communion likewise is a corporate act of the General Church for the reverent administration of which each autonomous Church is responsible to Christ alone. Members of the Free Churches in England and of the Church of Scotland often say that since Jesus Christ gave this sacrament to the whole Church the Church of England ought as a duty to admit to its celebrations of the sacrament any lovers of the Lord who wish to come. In fact Jesus Christ gave the sacrament into the keeping of the first apostles who established the Church and sketched out its first ministerial structures from which every Church derives its own tradition. The Church of England respects the structures of the Church of Scotland and the Free Churches as it respects the structures of the Church of Rome or the Greek Church. Members of other Churches ought in the same way to respect the Church of England in its guardianship and careful development of its own ministerial structures.

The Holy Communion wherever and however celebrated is always an act of worship and thanksgiving of the whole Church concentrated in its offering by the particular members of it there gathered together. They, whether many or few, have come to be partakers of this broken loaf and this cup of blessing; they are all visibly proclaiming before men the Lord's death and the Lord's resurrection. Agreement between different Churches on the meaning of the Eucharist can only be found by their taking as a starting point the biblical record of its institution; and none need go very far beyond that. Each Church will have its own tradition and liturgical method of celebrating

the Holy Communion with accompanying habits of cere-
monial. It is the duty of each Church reformed or un-
reformed to preserve its own tradition in so far as it is
adequate to its purpose and reverent in spirit, not hesitat-
ing to learn from the traditions of other Churches whether
by attraction or its opposite.[1]

It is for theologians and liturgiologists of each Church
to give account of its tradition and customs. The only
essential requirements for an orderly celebration of the
Holy Communion are a minister duly authorised in the
particular Church, a reverent consecration of the sacramental elements sufficiently presented before God for
their sacramental purpose, and a due taking, eating and
drinking by those who are there present. Each Church
sets its celebration in a liturgy of some kind or another;
all of which are derived in one way or another from the
early liturgies which have come down through the ages
with many embellishments, some enriching and some
obscuring or even in a manner disfiguring the central
purpose. There are many liturgically minded ministers of
religion labouring at present to bring the varied liturgies
of the different Churches to some single liturgical form or
shape which can serve all modern-minded congregations.
But a liturgy is essentially a domestic and intimate
possession of the Church which has fashioned it, its own
and no-one else's. In my own experience I have found
myself interested and enlightened and sometimes newly
inspired by the dissimilarities as well as by the similarities
between the traditional use of my own Church and that
of other Churches. In them all I find the same healthy

[1] When in Australia I found that leaders from the chief Churches were
engaged in drawing up a form of eucharistic liturgy which could be used by
all the Churches. I asked why, but got no answer. Such a liturgy would
necessarily be artificial and not domestic, home-grown.

intermingling of the pedestrian and the transcendent. Nor must it ever be forgotten that what one Church would consider numinous or congruous another would find unpleasing if not displeasing. The Church of England very rightly orders itself round one Book of Common Prayer for all its congregations.

Where Churches are in Full Communion there is free interchange between them of ministers and of communicants. That cannot be so between Churches not so related because of structural differences of faith and order between them which prevents it. Thus in these cases there arise the special problems concerning admission to communion by one Church of the communicants of another. These may be called problems of Sacramental Intercommunion to distinguish them from Intercommunion in general.

In the episcopal Churches baptism must be followed by episcopal confirmation before a member can be admitted to communicant status. There is however no uniformity between episcopal Churches as to the times or methods of confirmation and there are questions about its theology. The Commission on Anglican-Methodist relations has very rightly recommended that Full Communion could be established with the Church of England without any requirement from the Methodist Church that they should adopt episcopal confirmation. The Methodist and other reformed Churches do in fact have a ceremony by which members are received into full Church Fellowship: but there is no doubt that confirmation has had a necessary place in the initiation ceremonies from a very early date. It is a sign of grace that the Church of England while preserving the necessity of confirmation for its own members, does not regard it as an essential of Church order necessarily to be accepted along with episcopacy itself for Full Communion.

May an Anglican communicant receive the Holy Communion in a non-episcopal Church? He has always been at liberty to do so, in obedience to his own conscience; and there have always been those who did it: but it has so far been without official approval. Indeed Lambeth Conferences have been careful to say that 'it is the general practice of the Church that Anglican Communicants should receive the Holy Communion only at the hands of ministers of their own Church or of Churches in (Full) Communion therewith'. The Conference of 1930 recognised that in special missionary areas the bishop might explicitly depart from this practice. The Conference of 1968 gave more generous recognition to the freedom which inherently belongs to Anglicans, when it says that 'Anglican communicants may receive the Holy Communion in a non-episcopal Church as conscience dictates and when they know that they are welcome to do so'. This is to be 'under the direction of the bishop', and to apply only in Churches of good doctrinal standing; but while that is a right precautionary note, clearly each Anglican can in good conscience decide for himself in what is ultimately an entirely personal action.

But what about communicants of non-episcopal Churches receiving communion in an Anglican Church? Lambeth 1968 has brought to completion the process begun in Lambeth 1930. A non-episcopal churchman, if he or she has been duly baptised and is qualified to receive Holy Communion in his or her own Church may not only be 'received' but *welcomed* at the Lord's table in the Anglican Communion. This very properly has to be under the general control of the bishop in each diocese: but it is an alteration of doctrinal structure deliberately made to meet the pastoral needs of churchmen from other Churches and an alteration clearly required to meet the spirit of Christian unity, and one which can now bring increase of grace instead of controversy in parish life where there are mixed marriages.

Then there are the special occasions when groups or congregations of Anglicans and churchmen from other Churches, non-episcopal Churches, desire to take part together in a celebration of the Holy Communion as a special occasion different in scale or character from ordinary parochial occasions. It was not until 1933 that such a problem was beginning to present itself; and in that year the bishops of the Church of England passed similar resolutions in the two Upper Houses of the Convocation dealing with it. The Canterbury version was as follows:

> on special occasions, if and when they arise, when groups of members of the Church of England or of other Christian denominations are joined together in efforts definitely intended to promote the visible unity of the Church of Christ, the Bishops if requested may approve of the admission of baptised communicant members of these other denominations to Holy Communion according to the Anglican rite.

The bishops consulted with the Lower Houses but knowing that there would be great controversy if any attempt was made to give legislative effect to what was proposed, the bishops did not seek agreement from the Lower Houses, but left the resolution as one for the guidance of diocesan bishops in the exercise of their administrative discretion. By 1969 the climate had changed very greatly. At every assembly of the World Council of Churches there would be arranged a celebration of the

Holy Communion at which an Anglican bishop celebrated and all members of the assembly would be welcomed to communicate if they were able in conscience to do so. The same thing happened at very many smaller assemblies and conferences, which came nearer and nearer to the parish level. The 1933 resolution was clearly outdated, and clerical committees are engaged in drawing up a new regulation on more liberal lines to be put before the General Synod for approval in due course. The Lambeth Conference of 1968 introduced a new term and spoke of 'reciprocal acts of intercommunion'. The term is not well chosen, since it is not in the power of one Church unilaterally to regulate occasions of reciprocal acts. The new regulation should come under the heading of Sacramental Intercommunion, different from what is possible under General Intercommunion and more restricted than what is possible under Full Communion; and it would say what the Church of England allows or encourages for its own members under its jurisdiction. If occasions arise when the celebrant is not an Anglican or not in episcopal orders, it is not for the Church of England to issue directions and indeed it could not do so without causing misunderstandings: but each Anglican present at such a joint celebration would be able to obey his own conscience in the matter of communicating without hindrance.

In all these matters of intercommunion, and especially when administration of the sacraments is involved, the two essential requirements are firstly that each churchman should respect and conform to the directions or counsels of his own Church and secondly that each Church should make its own directions and counsels clear and charitable, being more careful of course where corporate actions are in question. And the saving grace is that each churchman has a divine right to follow his own conscience even against the advice of his own Church, though he must exercise that right with humility and good sense.

25

Marriage

IN or about 1937 the Bishops of the Church of England issued new regulations to govern the administration of the Marriage Discipline of the Church of England. It was not accepted by the Lower House of Clergy in the Convocations till twenty years or so later: but the bishops applied these regulations in their own dioceses on their own authority.

Beyond doubt Jesus Christ taught that in the will and purpose of God marriage should be the marriage of one man to one woman to abide together so long as they both should live. There should be no putting away of one partner by the other such as obtained in the Jewish religion and in both Greek and Roman practice. Every Church accepts this as the teaching of Jesus Christ. Most people in England, whether Christian or not, would agree that this is beyond doubt the ideal kind of marriage even if not always attainable. Every marriage conducted by the Church of England requires the partners to it to pledge themselves to lifelong marriage. In every civil marriage in England the registrar explicitly reminds the partners to it that it is commitment to a lifelong marriage.

The ancient rule of the Church was that the two partners contracted the marriage simply by their joint committing of themselves, their mutual 'troth' to one another: the priest was there to ratify and record the marriage and to bless it in the name of God. In every civilised country now the State sees to it that there is a legal record of every marriage. In England since the requirements of Canon Law and Statute Law are identical, its own registers suffice. The marriages conducted by any other religious bodies since they are not so bound to Statute Law, have to be certified by a registrar present in person.

No Church has any power to issue decrees of divorce. Only the State can issue decrees of divorce or of annulment, which is to declare that what was supposed to have been a marriage was for some legal fault or irregularity no marriage at all but null and void. The Church of Rome annuls marriages of its own members where the marriage was faulty or irregular by its own regulations; but this is only for its own denominational purposes, and any such annulment is of itself of no effect outside the Church of Rome's own jurisdiction. There are other peculiarities about the marriage discipline of the Church of Rome concerning mixed marriages between Roman Catholic and Anglican partners which, as it seems to the Church of England (and to many Roman Catholic theologians), are unjust and against the spirit which should govern all Churches within the General Church. But it is not necessary to say more about this matter here, urgent and important though it is.

Though the Churches do not issue decrees of divorce, the State does. It is right to do so since it would be wrong to deny to citizens who desire it some legal means of escaping from a marriage contract which has become intolerable to them: but the State will only grant a divorce in accordance with the requirements of its own divorce laws. The Church has no power or right to control the State's divorce laws: but all the Churches, as members of the community, have every right and every opportunity of giving Christian advice to Parliament and of making clear to it the dangers and possible disasters which would be inflicted on the corporate life of the nation by weak, over-permissive, unprincipled or otherwise bad divorce laws. If the nation were to abjure its official adherence to the principle of lifelong marriage or to abandon all efforts to protect it, the Churches would have to cease to recognise civil marriages as Christian marriages: but we have not yet got to that point. If it were ever reached, the Church of England would have to keep a separate register of marriages which it could recognise, and to set up its own courts for the granting of divorces or annulments. The Anglican Church in the U.S.A. has come near to setting up its own jurisdiction by giving its bishops power to disregard a marriage (which is in effect to annul it) if and when they think that in its origin the marriage was in some way an improper one by Christian standards. We might all come to something like that—but no one can regard as welcome the prospect of Church courts of this kind; and we know the danger which has been done to the reputation of the Church of Rome by its system of granting through its own ecclesiastical courts what to us look like divorces but are by them called annulments. Meanwhile by our teaching and practice we uphold and bear witness to the Christian principle of lifelong marriage.

And we do the same by refusing to marry in Church partners one of whom or both of whom have been divorced and have a previous partner still alive. To do so would offend against the principle of lifelong marriage and would violate the pledge contained in the marriage service to hold to one another 'till death us do part'. It should be made clear that the reason for refusing to marry is not that in their new marriage they would be 'living in sin' that is to say in a kind of adultery. They are proposing to do what is fully allowable by the law of the land and what may be thought in many cases a procedure fully justifiable to the conscience of a good Christian. To refuse to marry them in Church is in no sense a judgement upon them: it is thought by we of the Church of England a necessary thing if we are to keep clear and unmistakable our witness to Christ's principle of lifelong marriage.

Some clergymen and laymen want the Church of England to be willing to marry divorced people in Church, and I believe this has been or is to be allowed by our sister Church in Canada. Their reason is clear and respectable even though it may be thought very unwise. The advocates of this course think that the Church's witness to lifelong marriage can stand up in an adverse world without the support given to it by refusing to marry divorced people in Church: and so thinking, they wish to show full sympathy to those who are in good conscience marrying after a divorce and to give them full spiritual encouragement and help by marrying them in Church. I think they are mistaken in so thinking, and I ask myself how the Church is to discriminate fairly and effectively in the eyes of church people between those divorced people seeking marriage who can be rightly recognised as doing so in good conscience and those who cannot be so recognised. The Church could not possibly accept for marriage all divorced people in these days. I believe it is a safer and truer witness to lifelong marriage and its virtues to parents

and children alike to accept none: nor, as it seems to me,
should any Christian people feel aggrieved that it should
be so.

But that is not the only thing to be said to those who do
marry by a civil marriage after there has been a divorce
and who still have a previous partner living. The Church
has a personal, pastoral duty towards them. The Church
of England discipline now accepted throughout the
Church with full authority is that if people in this position
desire to continue as communicants (or to be confirmed
and become communicants) or if the parish priest wishes
to suggest such a course to them, he shall refer the matter
to the bishop who may at his discretion grant permission
on such conditions, if any, as he thinks it suitable to make.
This is thus treated entirely as a pastoral matter and the
parish priest or the bishop (and of course if necessary the
people concerned may apply direct to the bishop) acts
entirely as may seem best for the spiritual benefit of the
partners to the new marriage. One could say much more
on this point. I will only say that I operated this system of
discipline for twenty-five years or so in my own dioceses
and as Archbishop, also in the Army, Navy and Air Force
through the chaplains, that it worked easily and effectively
and without imposing any undue claims on my time, that I
operated it with scrupulous care, and that I am sure that
it brought great spiritual blessing to me in operating it
and to those for whose benefit I operated it. I can think
of no way of dealing with this particular pastoral problem
so rewarding in all ways as this. It is worth mentioning
specially that when it was introduced it was agreed among
the bishops that a decision made to approve of admission
to communion of such people by one bishop in his own
diocese would be honoured by all other bishops also.

I might add a word about the position of the Mothers'
Union. It has rendered grand service to the Church of
England over many years in a vast number of parishes,
and while bearing its witness to lifelong marriage, it has
done a work which could not be otherwise done in teaching church people to understand how to make the best of
family life and how to train children intelligently and
devoutly in Christian character and Christian faith.
Necessarily it could not accept to its membership women
who had been divorced or who had married divorced
men. In its work over the years it has had the enthusiastic
backing of the clergy, and indeed no parish can have a
branch of the Mothers' Union unless the parish priest
agrees. In recent times many clergy have demanded that
it should admit divorced women to membership, and
because it has not agreed have become hostile to it. This
is a poor return for what the Mothers' Union has done
and is still splendidly doing for the Church, for married
people and for the families of the Church. At a recent
World Conference (for the M.U. conducts a great deal of
admirable work through women trained and sent out by
it in Africa and India and elsewhere) when there was
considerable pressure from Anglo-Saxon Churches that
the rule be relaxed and divorced women be admitted, the
suggestion was heavily defeated by the representatives of
M.U. branches in Africa and India who said quite simply
that to do so would render all their work in creating a
Christian standard of married and family life in these
countries utterly futile. And of course so it would.[1] For

[1] Though the Lambeth Conference of 1968 has a resolution on Fellowship
for Church Women (30) and a resolution on Marriage Discipline (23) it
makes no reference to the Mothers' Union, to the remarkable work it has
done and is doing for the Church in England, or to the most valuable work
it is doing in Churches overseas, a regrettable omission.

this reason as well as for other reasons I hope that the Mothers' Union in England at least will not alter its rule or principles. They have never been more needed. At the same time I think it would be altogether good if the Mothers' Union could make some special arrangement by which divorced women who have been admitted to or continued in communicant status by the discretion of a bishop could be so associated with M.U. branches as to share fully in all the activities and privileges of membership. Thereby no injury would be done to the M.U. itself and valuable support would be given to the wise discipline of the Church of England in this matter.

26

Fact and Faith

THESE two words are like Siamese twins, inseparable and yet always distinguishable, though one is a matter of observation and the other of speculation. Fact refers to everything in our experience which is verified or verifiable or to be taken as such by scientific observation: faith is that in us which grasps the unseen and the unseeable and which lives in active endeavour towards its spiritual realisation in us. The Churches have always in their teaching put almost the whole emphasis on the unseen and spiritual, accepting without question the historic facts on which faith rests; and we must honestly recognise that Churches have in past days, when the nature and value of historical truth was not properly understood, in a spirit of reverence manipulated or manufactured history in order to support and stimulate the faith they wanted to teach. We live in an age of scientific observation, scientific discovery and careful evaluation of fact, which very properly put the whole emphasis on accurate definition of fact which they then interpret, illuminate and utilise according to the same scientific spirit. It must of course be understood that the scientific spirit is just as active and exacting in the study of theology or the other arts as it is in the study of the natural sciences. It must be understood also that scientific study would be a barren and futile pursuit if it were not again and again assisted and inspired by the free ranging spirits of imagination, poetry, fancy and intellectual speculation. But the basis of all knowledge must be scientific observation of fact. The time has therefore fully come when the Churches must go back to re-examine in the light of modern conditions of knowledge the faith which it teaches, to relate it afresh to the historic facts from which it first sprang and to see how far the free ranging spirits of piety or poetry, of philosophies or metaphysical speculations have inadvertently distorted or obscured the Christian message once delivered to the apostles. This is evidently a difficult and sometimes a painful task and not one that can be hurried. Private enterprise must go ahead making its contribution in reverent sincerity before the ruling bodies of a Church can give official approval to restatements of traditional ideas or disciplines. Bishops and clergymen must certainly be at liberty to contribute their own thinking to the evolution of sound doctrine, but since they are at the same time ministers of the Church they must have a special care not to disturb the peaceful working of the Church by rash speculation too little related to the permanent values of history. This total process has been long in operation. In or about 1938 a volume was published entitled *Doctrine in the Church of England*. It was a careful and judicious review of the doctrines of the Church of England worked out over fifteen years by a group of our best theologians, officially appointed to this work, under the chairmanship of William Temple. The second world war broke out very soon after, and the Church as a whole never really took up and seriously studied the report. If it had, church people would have been better equipped to meet the doctrinal conflicts of the post-war period. As it was, in the heat of meeting the new problems of Church unity and the first advances of oecumenicity, advocates of traditional theological concept were demanding another official commission on Church doctrine. That danger was averted. Only by a period, a confusing period, of trial and error can the Churches work their way through this exciting but disturbing advance to a faith securely based on facts of history and of observation, duly but not unduly illuminated by the graces of spiritual and poetic imagination. It is of the greatest significance that the Church of Rome which through the ages has relied less on historic investigation than on ideas of intellectual formulation and pious imagination regarded by it as divinely inspired and guaranteed, is now committed to this examination of its doctrines in the light of historic facts and of objective study of their meaning. Having made a good start in Vatican II, it seems now to be hesitant and in distress at the hardness of this hard road. We should have every sympathy with them as they face the kind of travail that the Church of England and other Churches first had to face four hundred years ago.

I venture to point to what is perhaps the greatest of all

areas of doctrine which have to be re-examined. The story of the crucifixion and all that led up to it is beyond all doubt, apart from possible inaccuracies (and not therefore to be disregarded) in minor details, historic fact concerning Jesus Christ the Man of God. It shows him reduced to complete impotence, utterly in the power of and at the mercy of, Jewish rulers and a Jewish mob—and then of Pontius Pilate. It was, strangely enough, Pilate who enabled Jesus Christ to explain to him in words the faith that was in him. To Pilate Jesus said that he was indeed a King, King of and in an invisible kingdom, with nothing to show as evidence of that kingdom except the plain fact that it was his own faithfulness to that kingdom which had brought him into his present state of complete impotence. The fact of the crucifixion was accompanied by this visibly impotent faith in the victim of it.

The faith of the disciples was that 'It is Jesus God raised up and of that we are all witnesses'. There is no kind of doubt that they believed that they had seen and spoken with the very Christ whom they had seen die on the Cross. There is no doubt that they believed that Peter and John had found the tomb empty. The New Testament gives some idea of what they meant by 'many infallible proofs' of the resurrection: and St. Paul had his own evidence. I believe utterly in the fact of the Resurrection of our Lord and in the fact of the empty tomb; but if anyone wishes to deny that it ever happened, or if anyone says he cannot build a faith on what may only be a vain imagination of excited followers of Christ, I cannot prove him wrong: nor can I prove that my belief in the resurrection is certainly founded on actual fact though evidently there is strong evidence to show that it did actually and historically happen, much as the Gospels say it happened.

But I have the strongest of all possible supporting evidence. Christ throughout his ministry preached about the kingdom of God. 'Seek ye first the kingdom of God', and everything else will fall into place. It is not untrue to say that he preached about nothing but God his Father 'in heaven' and the kingdom of God eternal 'in the heavens'. I believe daily more certainly in that kingdom not only because Christ proclaimed it, though that of course first gave me the idea, but because as life has gone on the Holy Spirit has been pointing out to me with ever increasing clarity and to my ever increasing conviction the reality and glory of the kingdom of God. This is of course not to shut one's eyes at all to the hateful evils in the lives of men and in the grim conditions that so often overwhelm them. But one shining example carries its own conviction against all contradiction. No one can possibly disprove the real existence of the kingdom of God which Christ preached: very few people really want to. They have a sneaking hope that something like it is true. Thus believing in the reality of the kingdom of God and in the trustworthiness of Christ who preached it, I welcome and rejoice in the resurrection not as an isolated fact but as an inevitable consequence fulfilling out of time and in God's world the final impotence of Christ revealed in time and among men. Christ gave all in his witness to the kingdom. God raised him from the dead. Thus the faith in the resurrection rests on verifiable fact—on the fact of his preaching and of his life and of his faith in God and increasingly on the fact of personal observation and experience.

Now that leaves the crucifixion to be just what it is, the evidence that in the last resort Jesus Christ himself could do nothing more for his kingdom than to suffer for it.

And here he puts himself on a level with every good man who finds himself impotent to help the good to overcome the evil and must be content to endure the evil. That brings Christ in impotence to the rescue of us in our impotence and teaches us true faith in the kingdom and encourages us to keep faith with it. This is a faith any can take to himself. Many are deterred from finding such a faith not least by the amount of theological, mystical, poetical and purely sentimental imaginings that have been heaped on the bare fact of the crucifixion and by their own reactions against some of these imaginings. The Church must surely unload a great deal of it from its teaching. Sin and death have not in any scientific way of thinking been overcome by the crucifixion though in the language of the kingdom of God they certainly have been. Though indeed it was through the sinful conditions of men and their endemic resistance to the call of the kingdom of God that the crucifixion came about, it is a false piety that supposes that in real fact it was for my sin or to release me from it that Christ suffered there. There was nothing which can properly be called vicarious about it. The purpose of Christ so far as we can relate it to ourselves was not primarily to save us from our sin but to help us to see the truth of God's kingdom and to show us how to remain faithful to the kingdom which he preached of God's love and forgiveness and renewal and victory through all misadventure and all suffering. The penitent thief had only just caught sight of the kingdom, but it sufficed.

I have tried to suggest that there is much unloading of accumulated pious thinking to be done. Last Good Friday (in Australia) I heard a very good sermon of the traditional kind on the Cross of Christ. It was clear, well expressed, very carefully worked out. It traced the course of human history from the Tree of Knowledge in the Garden of Eden and man's first disobedience through to the deliverance from the consequences of that sin wrought by Christ on the Cross to the vision to be found in the last chapter of the apocalypse of the Tree of Life, 'and the leaves of the tree were for the healing of the nations'. As we left the Church a good and well educated churchman who was with me said with a groan that he could not listen to a sermon which ignored completely the scientific fact of an evolution which did *not* begin from an original act of one man's disobedience. There is an immense appeal made today through music, drama and poetry to the fact of that death by which Jesus Christ knew that he could draw all men unto him. There is a real obstacle in the theological and pious ideas wherewith the spirit inherent in the Christ by whom men can be saved, has been overlaid and obscured. I incline to think that the greatest encouragement possible is being given to us of this day by the fact that neither the theologians nor the clergy are to be regarded now as solely responsible for the doctrine of the Church. Since it is now to be approved and understood also and equally by the laity, it must be stated in terms that they can understand, with the simplicity of Christ himself. So each Christian will clearly have to face for himself the spiritual reality and the spiritual crisis and the spiritual victory of the cross and the resurrection in his own living, unobscured by the complexities of scholastic thought forms.

them and as to what things he should pray for, for them or
for himself. Suggestions and advice from clergymen or
others in or out of church will be well intentioned and
may be helpful: but they may quite easily appear to
intrude unduly on privacy. I have always felt unhappy
when Roman Catholic authorities have exhorted Roman
Catholic people to pray 'for the conversion of England' to
the true faith. I have been disturbed when people barely
known to me have not hesitated to ask for my prayers for
them or for some project of theirs in what has become for
them no more than a pious habit of speech. I have been
disturbed when people openly working against some
endeavour of mine have in the same breath asked for my
prayers for them in endeavours of theirs. I have always
been very slow to ask other people to pray for me. Prayer
is not a thing to be snatched at or angled for. It is always a
secret thing which springs from friendship, God's friendship
with us and ours with him and with one another.

Many people are inclined by nature to talk freely and
at length to God about their private concerns or public
duties. God will bless them in it. There are many who do
not want to talk at length until they have something
which they want to talk over carefully, even word by word,
with God: and some can never be articulate before God
nor get beyond the simplest thoughts simply expressed.
Each must find his own pace and his own length. Christ
warned us all to avoid heaping up 'empty phrases as the
Gentiles do; for they think that they will be heard for
their many words'. That is a warning not to be neglected.

Private prayer is an occasional event: from my own
experience I should say necessarily a daily event, morning
and evening, in the course of what is the naturally prayerful life of a Christian. When St. Paul bade us 'pray without

ceasing' he meant that the Christian's spiritual attitude towards life must always be a prayerful attitude in that in it all, however absorbed he may be in his secular interests (and absorbed he should be) he is a servant of God called by Christ to be his friend. He is certainly not meant to be always occupied with conscious prayer. His life is always by its general character within the range of the kingdom of God and directed by its spirit, though at most times its activities and intentions are directed wholly to affairs belonging to this world.

A bishop said to me recently that of course prayer meant petition—asking for things. That is not at all my experience. There are times no doubt when petition predominates: but there is the collect to remind us that because of our unworthiness we dare not and for our blindness we cannot know what things we ought to ask for. Any petition we make must be made out of ignorance and always subject to 'if it be thy will'. Nor is prayer ever to be regarded as a protection against bodily danger or as a reserve resource to fall back on. It is always the lifting up of one's heart to God in sincerity and faith, whatever may be the circumstances attending it, whatever may be our prevailing mood at the time, and whatever may be chiefly occupying our minds at the time, as before God we remember and wonder and worry and rejoice and resolve and find a way, his way, to a provisional purpose and peace.[1]

I grew up in a home where naturally I learned the habit of daily 'saying my prayers', and I continued it throughout

---

[1] And then we recall the parable of the unjust judge (Luke 18:1) or of the importunate friend (Luke 11:5, coming immediately after the giving of the Lord's prayer). It is the joy of the Christian that as soon as he has got a thing straight and tidy on paper, there comes the sharp arrow from the Holy Spirit—but it does not apply to this person or in this case!

life because it had obtained for itself an essential place in my outlook on life. What I said and how I said it in my prayers remained always my own secret, and I learned little for the doing of it from advice from others or from books on prayer and almost everything from my own Christian common sense and faith. That is why my prayers remained always in sympathy with my understanding of God and of my duties and a constant discipline and strength to me. I have a feeling that Christians or near-Christians of today put less and less reliance on the habit of daily 'saying one's prayers' and consequently do not get the stabilising strength of will and purpose and faith that the practice of it can provide. Nor am I sure that the clergy are as anxious as they once were to encourage in these days among their people the faithful observance of this practice. Rather there is today an emphasis on corporate prayer in church and on the organised forms of such prayer which I feel to be somewhat unhealthy and in some cases domineering and intolerable. But it would not be in place for me to enter into a discussion here of the very complicated history of corporate prayer beyond what I go on to say about the Church of England's Book of Common Prayer.

28

The Book of Common Prayer

EVERY Church possesses some kind of provision for its common acts of corporate prayer. Forms authorised by a Church for this purpose are sometimes called liturgies, which mean public services of corporate worship.[1]

The Church of England Prayer Book has on its title page:

The Book of Common Prayer and administration of the Sacraments and other Rites and Ceremonies of the Church according to the use of the Church of England together with the Form and Manner of making, ordaining, and consecrating of Bishops, Priests and Deacons.

It dates from 1662 and is the only statutory Prayer Book which the Church of England possesses. The clergy at ordination and on subsequent occasions promise to use it in all statutory services of the Church and 'none other except so far as shall be ordered (i.e. 'arranged', not 'imposed') by lawful authority'. It is good to see it stated there on this title page that the rites and ceremonies contained in the book are 'of the Church' which is to say that they are of the Catholic Church, while being at the same time according to the use of the Church of England as a particular Church within the General Church. It underlines the truth that the Catholic Church of Christian faith is only to be found in action in its particular Churches and Communions.

[1] The description is dangerous. See St. John 4:21-24. It is difficult in public worship to preserve the quality both of spirit and of truth.

We owe to Cranmer the Prayer Book in the English language. The laity owe to him an even greater debt, seen especially in the provision of the services of Morning and Evening Prayer (Mattins and Evensong) together with a new arrangement of the service for the administration of the Holy Communion not only in English but in a greatly improved and literate style. These were to be the staple fare for the churchman's Sunday churchgoing, charged with all the spiritual insights newly apprehended at the time of the Reformation. They became a normal and familiar part of everyone's practice of the Christian religion and provided him (along with his English Bible) with his stock of religious ideas and with his spiritual vocabulary.

In the last century the Church came into disrepute because some of the clergy took the law into their own hands and made unauthorised and controversial alterations in the service of Holy Communion. At the same time, inadvertently, the development of choirs took away from the laity some of their co-operative share in the services (e.g. the saying of the psalms). Other strains and stresses came to bear on the language and ideas of the Book of Common Prayer. Early in the present century it was evident that the Book must be revised both that it might serve better the needs of the laity and that peace and good order might be restored to the public worship of the Church.

After great labour the Church produced the Revised Prayer Book of 1927 and presented it to Parliament. Parliament rejected it and also a second slightly amended version of 1928. This looked like a direct insult to the Church's right to order its own worship. So in a sense it was: but at the same time it was a godsend. It put an end to a bad relationship between Church and State and led

in due course to the present relationship of mutual consideration and co-operation where each party has a due
regard for the duties and interests of the other 'Establishment' at its best. The rejection was due chiefly to the fact
that both the ultra-catholic and the ultra-evangelical
forces in the Church of England and in the nation were
against the revised book though for opposite reasons: thus
it was made clear that more important than a revision of
the Book was a true reconciliation of these opposing forces.
By wise leadership from the bishops the crisis was sur-
mounted and all the best of the revisions made in the
Revised Book passed into the common use of the Church,
without statutory authority indeed but with the glad
goodwill of the bishops.

The Book of Common Prayer is the possession of the
whole Anglican Communion, one of its most precious
bonds of unity. It was the subject of a notable discussion
at the first Anglican Congress in Toronto (1963) after
which the Church of England had its first official Liturgical Commission. It belied the hopes which surrounded it.
Its first work was to produce a revised Service of Baptism,
with a considerable flourish of trumpets. This came before
the Convocations, suffered severely at the hands of
critics and was referred to a committee of which a
diocesan bishop was appointed chairman. So far as I know
it has never been heard of again. Revision was not such
a simple affair as it had appeared to the liturgiologists.

Meanwhile by means of a new Canon the Church had
obtained statutory powers by which the Convocations
could authorise revised services for experimental use in
the Church provided that they contained nothing contrary to or indicative of any departure from the doctrine
of the Church of England.

In due course the second Liturgical Commission produced amongst other services two revised services for the celebration of the Holy Communion, a Series I which was for the most part a combination of 1662 and the parts of the 1928 revision already in general use and a Series II which was designed as a new modernised alternative.

It is not my purpose to consider Series II in any detail; but I may make two general observations about it. It was not sent, as the earlier baptism service had been sent, by the Convocations to a committee for detailed examination. That might be thought a pity, since a Convocation committee might have been able to tidy up Series II in some respects and to reduce the vast number of permitted variations: but the omission was something more than a pity. It is at least possible that a large-scale revision such as Series II would raise questions of doctrine or questions containing doctrinal implications such as a committee of Convocation ought to have examined dispassionately. It caused me some surprise and distress when I discovered from the Liturgical Commission itself that in making the Series II service the Commission had only concerned itself with getting the shape of the service right and had not given any special attention to the doctrine or to the words. No wonder that in Convocation there was a very difficult debate on an important point of doctrine over a particular phrase in the proposed Prayer of Consecration. If Series II had been sent to a committee first, the unedifying piece of doctrinal disagreement and manoeuvring could have been avoided; and other points of possible doctrinal deviation could have been examined.

My second observation is to point to a difficulty which

arises over authorising such a service as one for the Holy
Communion for experimental use throughout the Church.
The extent of this experimental use is controlled in each
parish by the parish priest. Some of them to my knowledge
have taken the word 'experiment' to justify them in using
Series II in such a way as to discontinue over long periods
and at all the main services (if not entirely) the use of
Series I and of the main features of 1662 therein contained. Where that is done, it is likely that the people if
in the end asked for an opinion will support the giving to
Series II or something like it of full statutory authorisation,
simply because continued familiarity with it will have bred
acceptance: but the decision will have been made really
by the parish priest's control of the experiment. There is,
of course, the larger question. How far the laity in the
parishes are competent to form a wise judgement upon
details of liturgical form, whether it be details of doctrine
or of shape or of words, wherein any judgement is liable
to rest on nothing more solid than a 'taste' or a mood.
Certainly the laity would have been helped if the Convocations and the House of Laity had obtained a report from
a Convocation Committee appointed to examine the ideas
of the liturgiologists both in respect of doctrine and with
regard to the suitability of its general use in the parishes
as a vehicle for conveying the teaching and the spirit of
the Church of England.

No one is likely to question the fact that there must
be a duly authorised revision: but in my view the one
thing not to be lightly or wantonly surrendered is the
possession by the Church of England of one Order for the
administration of the Holy Communion with which every
communicant and congregation at the Holy Communion
is thoroughly at home, and the wording of which is familiar

and notably memorable.[1] Without that this Church of England can never be 'a city at unity in itself'.

There is another consideration. In Canada, the U.S.A., Uganda, Kenya, and Australia, in all of which countries I have been recently, I find the Communion Service (whether in English or not) if revised at all, still so close to our moderate revisions of the 1662 Order that I can easily follow it and can use it without any difficulties when I celebrate with it. The differences are so small and simple that one can take them in one's stride—but that is not true of Series II. There is thus a sad loss to the whole Anglican Communion.

The Lambeth Conference of 1958 first discussed the general subject of Prayer Book Revision and indicated how the subject should be tackled. Yet at the Lambeth Conference of 1968 no attention was given to the subject, and no account given of what had been done in various parts of the Anglican Communion. Thus for the Communion in general and the Church of England in particular (where perhaps it is most needed) no guidance comes from the Lambeth Conference.[2]

[1] There could of course be provision for a shortened Order of the one service when it is necessary to save time: but the Order itself should be one that all can grow to understand and appreciate.

[2] I did not find in any of the Provinces of the Anglican Communion any active interest in the subject of Prayer Book revision; in Australia there seemed to be no interest at all. Inevitably the initiative and the pressure for action comes from above upon the clergy and the laity.

29

Holiness

THIS, far and away the most important of all these chapters, must also, if it is not to miss the point, be one of its shortest. The word holiness has many different meanings or implications and suggests many very different images. Here I point to one meaning only and that the one essential meaning which it must have for every Christian. St. Peter puts it in the fewest possible and most pregnant of all words. Having pointed us to the 'living hope' to which we are born again through the resurrection of Jesus Christ from the dead, he goes on to say:

> Therefore gird up your minds . . . As obedient children, do not be conformed to the passions of your former ignorance, but as he who has called you is holy, so be ye holy in all your daily behaviour: for it is written, You must be holy; for I am holy. And if you call on him as Father who judges each one, without respect of persons, according to his works, conduct yourselves during the time of your dwelling here, in fear.

Godly love and godly fear are two sides of the same coin. Love is without form among men until it has taken shape in responsibility. Holiness is to be found only in the activities of persons who recognise their responsibilities, both in their range and in their limitations. That is the lesson of Christ's incarnation and distinguishes the Christian meaning of holiness from all other uses of the word, sacred or profane.

The Church in general has through the ages tended to treat holiness as a special grace of the sanctuary, of the sacred, of the saint, standing away from ordinary men at the ordinary levels of Christian experience. In Christ's religion, as St. Peter underlines, holiness is the possession of all Christians called as such, by baptism, to be saints,[1] as they conduct themselves in the home, the office, the market place, the factory, in all sorts and conditions of work and leisure. Holiness therefore is essentially the possession of persons, an expression of each person's character and performance. Like truth or love or unity, holiness cannot be the characteristic of a thing or of a society, not even of a Church except in a secondary sense. In that sense it still has a real significance and value in the affairs of men: but inevitably it lacks that virtue of single mindedness which belongs to a person by virtue of his being himself and nobody else. The Church, as the household of God, has its constant duty of teaching and training the members of the family in the ways of righteousness and in the joys of holiness. Each Church, as a household, has its own atmosphere, tradition, pattern of Christian life in its keeping or rather in the keeping of its appointed ministers; its own ideas of holiness. No Church has anything but an imperfect record in its family history in this respect, and with too many skeletons in the cupboard. No Church is without its family honours and achievements. But the kind of holiness which God requires is personal holiness in the members of the Church each of whom he is calling to be an inheritor of eternal life.

Just at present the Churches in Vatican Councils, Lambeth Conferences, and Oecumenical Councils are proclaiming that the service of the Church to the world must be discharged mainly by the laity. It is equally and

[1] *Hagios* (Greek), *Sanctus* (Latin) (from which Saint) and Holy (English) are equivalents in meaning.

profoundly true that the service of the Church to God must be discharged mainly by the laity. It is the grievous fault of clerical self-centredness that bishops and clergy have been so slow to recognise that this is the real meaning of 'collegiality' and 'co-responsibility'. The common grace which clergy and laity alike need for their witness to God and to the world is holiness, interpreted in the full light of the revelation of Christ, the characteristic virtue of the kingdom of God lived out by Christian people as best they can in the circumstances of their earthly condition, by trial and error, by faith and unfaith, by evil report and good report, by the witness of word and deed. I have said enough to point to the goal of all Christian striving—not holiness, not piety as generally understood, nothing eso-teric or withdrawn, but a holiness which is a lively expres-sion of faith and works in a man's, a woman's behaviour in the affairs of daily life, and in every occupation sacred and secular alike.

Words from the Book of Common Prayer come to my mind:

> . . . And to all thy people give thy heavenly grace; and specially to this congregation here present; that with meek heart and due reverence, they may hear and receive thy holy Word; truly serving thee in holiness and righteousness all the days of their life.

And:

> . . . we beseech thee, give us that due sense of all thy mercies, That our hearts may be unfeignedly thankful, and that we show forth thy praise, Not only with our lips, but in our lives: By giving up ourselves to thy service, And by walking before thee in holiness and righteousness all our days.

30

Church and State

THE Church of England has always been a serving Church, ministering to this nation as the times made possible or required, and always (except for a brief period when it was dispossessed) under the unifying and sanctifying authority of the Monarchy. It fell to me in my office as Archbishop of Canterbury to administer to Queen Elizabeth II the oath by which she bound herself before God to rule her peoples faithfully and in accordance with the laws of the country; and then to anoint and crown Her Majesty according to a form of service which goes back in its main features to the beginnings of the British Crown and long before that to Byzantium and to Jerusalem, bearing witness to the faith that Sovereign and people are bound together in a common loyalty to God and to one another. History shows, I think, that if that golden chain of loyalties is broken or abused, a power and a virtue goes out of the life of a nation beyond recall.

This country has no written constitution: nor does the Church of England have a written constitution governing its position as the Established Church. The health of the country rests on an understanding between Sovereign, Parliament and people, with the Church as the servant of all: the duties of its position change as the times change. The Church has in its time been unduly subservient to all. It is thought by some that the last instance of such undue subservience was when the Church had to accept the rejection by Parliament of its revision of its Prayer Book, though as I have said the rejection proved in the end to have been a boon. Since then, as it has seemed to me, the relationship has become more and more one of mutual understanding and helpfulness. Parliament has no desire any longer to control the spiritual affairs of the Church: but it has an overseeing duty to see that any Church measure which it is asked to approve is in proper legal shape and does not prejudice any of the legitimate interests of Her Majesty's subjects. That is a very proper form of control for Parliament to exercise and it is a real benefit to the Church to know that its Measures will have to be subjected to that kind of scrutiny.

There is the matter of Crown appointments of bishops and others. I can say that in my time there too what was subservience has become an honourable and helpful partnership. The Sovereign appoints on the recommendation of the Prime Minister. The Prime Minister recommends only after close consultation with the relevant Church authorities. As regards the appointment of diocesan bishops, no one is recommended to the Crown who was not in the first instance proposed for nomination to the Prime Minister by the two Archbishops. Before any such proposal is made to or considered by the Prime Minister, the Archbishops have made their own enquiries in the search for suitable names for that particular diocese. On his side the Prime Minister has caused expert enquiries to be made from Downing Street. The two sets of enquiries, discreetly made from many representative clergymen and laymen, are kept in touch by frequent discussion between them. Finally a short list of names, generally three, is submitted by the Archbishop of the Province concerned to the Prime Minister who then selects from it. The Church at large can be satisfied that the

Archbishops have done everything in their power to secure that each person whose name is on the short list is a suitable person for appointment to meet the needs of that particular vacant diocese and that they can find no others more suitable. Other Churches have other ways of managing the selection of persons for appointment as diocesan bishops. It is my own judgement that no other system of selection is superior to or as good as ours in the care with which it is worked, the great efficiency and dignity of its working, or the general success of its results.[1]

There have been many critics of the establishment as in some way a threat to or a domination of the spiritual liberties of the Church, or as the Scottish Presbyterian says 'of the Crown rights of Christ over his Church'. There have always been a few members of the Church Assembly to raise the issue again and again. There have been many commissions appointed to review the situation. Some of the enthusiasts have seen to it that the issue was introduced into the discussions of the Anglican-Methodist Commission on Union though it was not relevant to the particular question of achieving Full Communion. It is notable that in a recent report on discussions between the Church of England and the Church of Scotland, the representatives of the Church of Scotland went on record as saying that they had no fault to find with the existing system of the Establishment of the Church of England.

One may confidently say that the attitude of the Free Churches has changed enormously in the last fifty years or so. Then there was a passionate cry for disestablishment. Now, with true friendship established between the

---

[1] This system rests throughout on the wise exercise by all concerned of discretion, and of course right up to the final decisions discretion may be at fault. Busy people in all aspects of public life are driving us all to think that the public weal will suffer unless everyone has a right to be consulted.

Churches instead of rivalry and conflict, the Free Churches have discovered that the Establishment has positive advantage both for them and for the country as serving well the whole place of the Christian religion in the life of the nation. United now in a common service, they find it a real strength to all the Churches to have the historic Church of England to lead them in that common service to Christ and to the country. Thus they have in fact become part, a real and active part, of the Establishment themselves. And I can see in some of my Roman Catholic friends a similar feeling.

At the end of the service of the Coronation of Queen Elizabeth II, as we were dispersing in the annexe to the Abbey, a distinguished Baptist minister said to me in words which deeply moved us both: 'Archbishop, thank you for what you have done for us all. Only the Church of England could have done it.'

To avoid misunderstanding, I must add one further paragraph. If secular authority asks the Church for its opinion on some subject, it must of course given an authoritative answer. Thus when the Government asked Archbishop Davidson for an opinion on the proposal for a fixed Easter, he (having made such consultations as he thought were appropriate) replied for the Church of England that so long as the other main Churches were ready to accept the idea of a fixed Easter the Church of England would be. If my recollection is right, other Churches said much the same except the Church of Rome which declined to give any decisive answer. I believe that now it has expressed its willingness to agree. The situation is more difficult when members of the Church of England itself (or the authorities of this or any other Church) state as though with authority their decision or doctrine or

mand about particular or general doctrinal or political
questions.[1] The bishops may come to think that an answer
for one reason or another not opportune or that for lack
of sufficient discussion or sufficient agreement an answer
or an adequate answer is not possible. Here the Church
of Rome is in a very special difficulty. Vatican Council II
brought a number of doctrinal issues into the sphere of
open discussion; it also obtained for the bishops of the
Church of Rome a position of doctrinal co-partnership
with the Pope. One of the issues of immediate importance,
doctrinal and political, is that of the planning of parent-
hood. On this an episcopal commission, appointed by one
Pope and strengthened by the present Pope made a report
to the present Pope who then rejected its advice and
published an encyclical, *Humanae Vitae*, forbidding the
use of contraceptives as a violation of God's natural laws.
He thereby brought to a head two issues on which bishops
and theologians of the Church of Rome are in fact sharply
divided. Is the Pope's judgement on the doctrinal issue
right or wrong? Is the Pope's demand that his judgement
must be obeyed because he as Pope has given it right or
wrong? The same dilemma presents itself in the Discussion on Holiness and Celibacy in which the Pope is
involved.

Strangely enough history has something to teach us
here. The Churches of Asia Minor had preserved the most
ancient of all methods of fixing the date of the Easter
festival. When the Easter festival was introduced at Rome
(c. A.D. 160) another reckoning of the date was followed.
About A.D. 190 Bishop Victor of Rome, finding that

---

[1] It is as difficult now as it ever was to make a clear distinction between
what are purely doctrinal questions and what have political implications of
more or less pronounced character.

Christians from Asia Minor living in Rome were following their own traditional custom, forbade them to do so and demanded conformity in the observance of Easter with Roman usage, a demand which the Churches of Asia Minor regarded as autocratic and offensive. In the year A.D. 664 at a synod held at Whitby at which the Church in the North of England agreed to submit itself to government from Rome, the Church was also persuaded to abandon the Eastern method of calculating the date of Easter and against all its conservative instincts to accept the Roman method of dating Easter. In a recent book on *The Early Church*[1] it is said that 'Pope Victor apparently believed that the Roman custom must have been inherited from the instructions of Peter and Paul, and declared that those who observed the feast on any different day could not be regarded as Catholic Christians'. The author also says that 'there can be little doubt that the Quartodecimans (those who followed the Eastern custom) were right in thinking that they had preserved the most ancient and apostolic custom. They had become heretics simply by being behind the times'. There are morals in this bit of ancient Church history for those who consider the relationships of the Church and State if on either side tendencies towards absolutism appear.

The Early Church by Henry Chadwick, Regius Professor of Divinity at Oxford. Pengiun Books, pp. 84–85 and p. 256.

31

The Church and the World

IN the next section of this essay, I shall be looking at the role of the Christian in the life of the world of which he is a part. Here I want to say a brief last word about the Church as it confronts the world. As the last Lambeth Conference said most truly, 'The role of the Church in the world is the role of her Lord: that of the suffering servant'. In an early chapter I said that the great purpose of our Lord in his incarnate life was to point to, to exhibit so far as it can be exhibited in a human life, and to authenticate, the existence and the character of the kingdom of God. It is an inevitable part of the Church's ministry to suffer for the truth's sake. It is an essential part of the Church's ministry to take care that it is to the utmost of its power a good and faithful servant, learning in the whole of its ministry to enter into the joy as well as the sorrows of its Lord. It must know that every day of its ministry is a day of the Lord's coming and a day of judgement. Yet it is part of its ministry, as it was of our Lord's ministry, to make friends with men of the world by means of the coinage of this world, not forgetting that sometimes the sons of this world are wiser in their own generation than the sons of light. The Church is 'to make prayers and supplications, and to give thanks, for all men'.

All through its history the General Church and every part of it has felt acutely its lack of power and has been seduced into bad ways by its desire for more political power, often for use towards quite virtuous ends. Christ

6

in the days of Holy Week was aware of a total lack of any power except the power of the Holy Spirit; he never allowed himself to be seduced for a moment into a snatching at any kind of temporal power, even to save himself. Here is a parable of the kingdom which no churchman must ever allow himself to forget.

In these days the multiform powers of 'the world' organised as they are in so many ways and with such frightening efficiency and effrontery menace the Church in so many ways and obscure in so many ways the things of the Spirit. The Church is specially engaged at present in girding up its strength both for its conflict for truth and even more for its mission to bring succour to the poor, the under-privileged, the sufferers from cruelty and injustice, the sinful. All these are 'world' problems and the Church feels challenged to meet them with all the resources of a 'world' Church. And yet this laudable purpose leads the General Church and each particular Church into great temptation as they organise themselves after the pattern of this world's organisations. There is no other pattern suitable for the purpose: but Our Lord before Pilate said, 'My kingship is not of this world'.

Organs of unity, of corporate fellowship, of common thought and co-ordinated purposes there must be in the Churches: but there are inherent dangers in such unifying concepts. Writing of the Future of Man, a modern prophet Pierre Teilhard de Chardin speaks of 'The Collectivisation of Mankind' as an irresistible physical process and, as an inductible part of that physical process, of the evolution and maturing of a collective consciousness of all mankind living and dead. 'Without the evolution of collective thought' he says 'through which alone the plenitude of human consciousness can be attained on earth, how can there be a consummated Christ'.[1] Thus he reaches out deliberately towards St. Paul's image of the Church and all mankind growing to their mature manhood in Christ as Christ himself grows to his perfection as the Perfect Man wherein is seen the plenitude not only of man but of Christ and of God. This solution of all creation in 'the physical primacy of Christ and the moral primacy of Charity'[2] may be the great vision men need to unite the scientific and the spiritual understanding of creation: but it is a far cry from the gospel of Christ, uniting men and women through their personal apprehension, by and of the love of God, to the kingdom of God which Christ reveals and which we are to seek. It has always been my instinct to keep my feet on the ground, while my eyes can watch the path before my feet and scan the distant horizons, but can most of the time observe what lies in the middle distances. It has seemed to me that in recent times those who speak for the Church and to the Church are too much concerned with cosmical ideas, with concepts of plenitude, with magnitudes of organisation and of outlook, and fall into the error of regarding oecumenical ambitions and ideologies as the divinely appointed instruments by which and by which alone the Church's evolution in truth, unity and godly love can be accomplished.

I have been concerned in this second part of this essay to emphasise what seems to me to be some necessary parts of the equipment of a churchman of any Church—that the General Church of Christ Militant here on earth is only observable in the operations of the particular autonomous Churches; that each particular Church so long as it wishes to preserve its own separate identity must bear its

[1] *The Future of Man* by Pierre Teilhard de Chardin.
[2] *Ibid.*, p. 94.

own burden of responsibility for what it contributes to the witness and mission of the General Church; that part of its burden is so to pay due respect to all other Churches as not to seek any pre-eminence but only the edification of the General Church in love; that its first duty is to teach and help all its members in the way that they should go towards the kingdom of God in spirit and in truth; and that to this end it should seek to be in the spiritual unity of Full Communion with all other autonomous Churches. And here again, each Church must be very careful about what it says officially to the world or to its own members. The Church of Rome must be especially careful what it says through the Pope or otherwise, concerning Church doctrines, Christian duties or Church conduct in political affairs, just because, though the Papacy may no longer claim direct control over the temporalities of human affairs it does still, directly or indirectly, make the assumption of some kind of general responsibility for the direction of all human affairs. The Churches have the right and often the duty of giving advice to the authorities of this world: but in discharging this difficult and sometimes dangerous duty, they must never allow themselves to forget that every churchman has the inalienable right and the frequent duty to form his own judgements and to obey them in the interrelated spheres of temporal and spiritual responsibilities. The voice of the Church must in all circumstances be the voice of grace, wisdom and understanding, a reconciling voice, reconciling men to God and to one another: for 'God was in Christ reconciling the world to himself and entrusting to us the message of reconciliation'.

PART THREE:

CHRISTIANS IN THE WORLD

32

The World

In New Testament times, to become a Christian meant to be baptised into the Church. Then and now churchmen owe this loyalty both to the Gospel of Christ and to the Church of Christ. But it is no longer possible or desirable to give such a precise and restricted meaning to the word Christian. It may be said legitimately now that those who feel some kind of personal loyalty, if not to Jesus Christ himself, yet to the kingdom of God which he preached and to the quality of behaviour which it requires of them are in some sense Christians. Churchmen and Christians alike are led into temptation daily by the fact that they are also men and women of the world; and the word temptation means a constant testing of the sincerity and truth of their loyalties to the kingdom of God.

In this context the world must be distinguished completely from the natural world and from the natural universe as studied by the scientist. For the Christian the world means primarily and ultimately the men and women in it.

'So God loved the world, that he gave his only begotten Son, to the end that all that believe in him should not perish, but have everlasting life.' No Christian can love the world as God loved and loves it. Only God can love like that. We saw earlier that for we men love is without form and void until it expresses itself in a sense of responsibility. By his sense of responsibility a person is related to another or to others, to them and therefore for them and with them also. The incarnation of Jesus Christ related the love of God in responsible action to, for, and with the world of men. To Christ we say, 'Thou that takest away the sins of the world, have mercy upon us'. The world put Christ to death. His crime was preaching and living according to the kingdom of God. Thereby he was made a criminal by the world, and by accepting the worldly consequences liberated everyone who desires liberation from the tyrannous servitudes of sin and death. No Christian can ever do the service for the world which Christ did, though he may and indeed in his own measure must take his share in that service.

Each Christian has to decide for himself in which particular world or worlds out of all the possible worlds before him he will serve God. He can try to narrow his world to his own family or to his own social or business group; or to his own colour; he can try to live the unsubstantial life of a cosmopolitan.[1] But there is one 'world' from which we cannot detach ourselves, the 'world' of our own nation to which we belong. It is the fact, at times the unpleasant fact, imposing on us conditions and obligations. Englishmen can count themselves fortunate in that they have a national history reasonably continuous and coherent from its beginnings to this present day, invaded only twice from outside, once by imperial Rome and once by the Norman invasion led by William the Conqueror and declared by the Pope of that day to be a Crusade.

[1] One must mention with special respect and honour men and women who choose or are chosen to lay aside their own personal and national interests and selflessly to serve the causes of international or supranational truth, unity and godly love. Pre-eminent among such persons the Church must always place Christian missionaries who give their lives to the service of the Church in foreign countries in answer to a Christian vocation: but inevitably this kind of cosmopolitan service carries with it its own special temptations.

In trying to assess the place of Christians in the world, we shall be wise to start at every point from the vantage point of our own place as citizens of the English nation, with all the advantages, disadvantages and obligations thereby incurred.

33

The National Character

DR. Mandell Creighton, once Bishop of London and a great one, got into trouble on one occasion by saying that he was an Englishman first, and a churchman second. It is obviously in the order of time entirely true. His baptism into the Church came after his birth into the world. It is also true spiritually. Each one of us is influenced profoundly for life by the environment into which we are born and in a general sense by the nation into whose citizenship we are born. One need do no more than note the differences between Scotsman, Welshman, Irishman and Englishman—or looking at a far more troubled part of the world, between the Jordanian Arab and the Israeli Jew.

In England there are so many different kinds of citizen, so differently grouped and classed that it is not possible to give any really accurate account of our national character: but yet most of us have a kind of idea of what we mean by it. Through history and all its vicissitudes, there is a certain element of continuity which can be felt to be part of our national character, a kind of character made up of a multitude of varied ingredients which however much the proportions of the ingredients change, still reveals enduring characteristics.

In an Australian paper commenting on the Budget statement made in April, 1969, I saw a quotation from a financial writer who had said: 'recent years have witnessed a progressive debasement of the British character . . . The desire to serve the public interest has declined sharply.' The decline is said to be in the ordinary citizen's desire to serve the public interest: but except at moments of crisis, the desire of the ordinary citizen in this country to serve the public interest has never, I think, been very high. On the other hand save when overborne by some idealistic appeal, the obstinate determination of the ordinary citizen to fight for what he imagines to be his individual rights has never been higher than it is now. Only the methods of fighting have changed and the possible methods of serving the public interest have changed too. The real change between this and earlier days is that behind every short-sighted or selfish or bad cause is now arrayed organised support a great deal more clever, seductive and compelling than the quiet forces which make for wisdom and for healing. Competition is made ruthlessly cut-throat and drives out of the field altogether the gentle arts of co-operation and reconciliation and constructive skill. Shall we still find faith in the British character? Shall we still put our trust in British skill and competence? Yes, indeed: and those who have eyes to see, can see plenty of evidence of both all round them in our quietly sensible and loyal citizens both young and old. 'In quietness and confidence shall be your strength' said Isaiah to the citizens of his time. But it is more than ever necessary that all Christians should take the utmost care to see that to the best of their respective abilities they lay aside private and party prejudices and seek to form sound judgements on their current affairs whether in their own families and their own affairs or in the family of the nation. The constant endeavour to do this is good exercise of our moral faculties, a constant education of our intelligence, an exacting and exhausting test of endurance and a 'praying without ceasing'.

It may be said that there is no purpose in so doing since it makes no difference to the course of events: still good will suffer and evil will triumph. It is at this point that we must remember the proper limitations which are part of our Christian profession. To say that we must love God and love our neighbour and to stop there is foolish. Love means a sense of responsibility; but each one of us can only carry his own burden of responsibility, measured by the limits of his own reach, his own abilities and the opportunities given to him. On every issue the Christian must try to discover both the merits of the matter so far as it concerns him as a citizen and the dimensions of his own responsibilities in the matter. Humble and devout prayers of a general kind are never out of place. But the test comes always in the particular decision, which lies directly within the range of our own responsibilities and possibilities.[1]

In the following chapters I try to analyse in some particular instances how we can attempt to clear our minds as to what a Christian's range of responsibilities may be.

---

[1] Thus each Christian is called to the solemn vocation of being himself, bearing his own burdens—yet he cannot be himself in isolation. He is made and called to be a member of a society and of societies. But all societies including the Church lead him into manifold temptations.

34

Action

BEHAVIOUR is action of a sort. How you behave depends upon how you believe. Your behaviour reveals your moral self. The word morality is so overloaded with overtones that it can hardly be used without creating misunderstandings. Another word for the same thing is ethics: but the word sounds somewhat stiff and sophisticated. Anyhow whether one speaks of behaviour or morals or ethics, one is speaking always of what belongs to persons and reveals to other persons what they can see of their worth. There are many codes of morality and systems of ethics and kinds of behaviour: but to Christians and non-Christians alike the real interest is in the character of each person and of his personal behaviour. Though there be codes many and standards many, each person is himself answerable for his own action. If a person has one standard of morality as a politician and another as a business man and a different one as a parent and friend, he has not established that there are so many different codes of morality; he has only demonstrated that he is not single minded, but adapts his behaviour to suit his surroundings. He is not an integrated person: he has no integrity.[1] As St. James once said, such a man lacks wisdom; is like a wave of the sea that is driven and tossed by the wind. 'Let not that man think that he shall receive anything of the Lord. A double-minded man is unstable in all his ways.'

[1] When Lord Attlee died, it was noticeable that the one characteristic of his stressed in all references to him was his integrity.

A responsible citizen, a responsible Christian must have consciously or sub-consciously some kind of pattern of seemingly wise action by which he regulates his whole response to life. What kind of pattern is it to be? To express adequately the citizen's intricate patterns would take a volume and would still be inadequate: fortunately the Christian's pattern can be put more succinctly.

Once an impetuous man came running to Jesus Christ and kneeled to him and asked him, 'Good Master, what shall I do that I may inherit eternal life?' There was another occasion when the people said to Jesus Christ, 'What must we do, to be doing the works of God?'. On both occasions the people concerned wanted a guide to action. 'What shall I do?' 'What must we do?' In every call to action the Christian must have regard to the two aspects with which he has to deal—my individual action, our co-operative actions; and for the Christian the objective is one and the same—in every action to the best of his ability and within the possibilities of his situation to glorify God and to serve his kingdom. Thus both his individual and his co-operative responses in action are equally related to his knowledge and love of God.

But in all his actions the Christian is also a man of the world in general, a citizen of his own country in particular, and here in this country a citizen of England, affected by the national character and making his own small contribution to its development or decline. As we go on to consider some of the calls to such individual and co-operative action which confront us in our national life, it will suffice to speak in a general way of the kind of judgements required of each one of us in our daily avocations as citizens of a nation whose prevailing culture is by tradition Christian. Our question will be—what line of action is the right line for an ordinary citizen of this country to take who is reasonably intelligent, generally disposed to be a respectable and responsible member of society and so far Christianly inclined. No committed Christian will forget that it is his care and concern not only to satisfy the moral demands which society makes upon him as citizen and Christian but also to seek earnestly in all things to go beyond them in the service of Christ. St. Paul ends a passage dealing with a Christian's social duties with the words 'Do not be overcome by evil, but overcome evil with good', a positive call to a spiritual militancy.

35

Individual Action

WHATEVER a citizen of this country may do, he is inevitably affected by his English environment, by members of his family, by his friends and by public opinion. Even so he remains in his own eyes and in the sight of others an individual person, with his own individual freedoms of judgement, of decision and of lawful action. He is in an important sense a free man, a member of a free community possessing certain personal rights and owing to the community certain ascertainable duties.

In particular he has his own personal responsibility for those moral decisions by which he both shapes and reveals his personality. It is very true that some of his moral decisions may be forced upon him rather than chosen by him by the nature of his work, by professional etiquette or by obedience to an accepted ideology. In any case issues of personal morality are often hard to decide clearly, and a decision when made is often difficult to carry through wholeheartedly or at all. But even so we all recognise that each one of us retains his own relative freedom and relative responsibility over a wide area of his moral life of purpose and decisions. In this wide area, the citizen has his own pattern of preferred moral choices and moral actions. That is the kind of person he is in the community. How is this controlling pattern to be formed?

It is true, I think, to say that by most citizens it is formed with the minimum of introspection. It grows unnoticed and mostly without direct control. That is, of course, why in the community, things so easily go wrong. At a time like this when acceptance of a norm of moral standards is so uncertain and so unstable, it is incumbent upon every citizen, to ask whether there is or ought to be some general pattern of personal moral behaviour which should command general respect. Though it is rarely referred to publicly, there is in fact a generally observed pattern, the one that is observed or at least encouraged and desired by ordinary decent families for their own lives and for the communal life. Positively it may be described as a pattern of generosity of spirit tempered by a tinge of puritanism: negatively as a pattern not disfigured by stealing, lying, quarrelling, covetousness, concupiscence, domineering and the like. We all distrust and dislike people guilty of such habits of behaviour in our own circle. Yet it is not to be denied that in public life generally behaviour of this kind, decently disguised or excused is applauded and rewarded. Each citizen is one moral person, responsible in his own life to one general pattern of moral behaviour. How is he to be rooted and grounded in this pattern of good and generous citizenship, if in the public life of the country it gets no more than lip service if that? Only if all those who take an influential part in public life, men working by hand and eye and pen will examine their own personal standards of behaviour, define to themselves what good morality and good citizenship demands of them positively and negatively and then to the best of their ability honour and obey this pattern of behaviour in all their activities, in the home, their circle of friends, in their public life.

Is there such a pattern to be found operative anywhere? Most certainly. Clear elements of it are to be found in the honouring or dishonouring of them in every home where the mother is trying sensibly to discipline or house-train and family-train her children. But in very many homes training of this sort is done feebly and is done badly or not at all. The right pattern is to be found presented and honoured in every school in the country with more or less effectiveness. Whatever else is being taught, from the head teachers down to the most junior member of the staff all are bound to keep order and teach order, which is to instil into the pupils their first ideas of orderly behaviour in public, the first principle of good citizenship. There cannot be order without obedience; there cannot be good order without ample room within the order for personal initiative properly displayed. Every head teacher knows that and does his or her best to instil such a pattern of behaviour in every pupil in order that they may grow up into good citizens and do credit to our national character.

One hears censorious adult citizens sometimes complaining that the nation spends millions of the citizens' money on schools and judging from the behaviour of their ex-pupils there is nothing much to show for the money after all. It is still not realised that if the results of all this school training in citizenship seem disappointing, the fault is least of all with the schools. It is the fault of a vast number of adult persons who are failing to order their own individual actions in such a way as to uphold, illuminate and adorn this desired pattern of national character. It is the fault of those mothers and fathers who do not know what good order in the family life is or how to achieve it; it is the fault in some schools and places of higher education that some students and some of those appointed to teach them have allowed their own kinds of covetousness and concupiscence suitably rationalised to abolish their natural generosity of spirit and their natural deference to one another and to destroy good order; it is the fault of a great number of adults in all walks of life who in their adult occupations allow themselves to accept or to promote a pattern of behaviour the same in essentials as that of schoolboys who have not yet learned the meaning of good order nor the arts of bringing all the virtues of individual initiative into generous service of the community and the common good.

What is needed is beyond all doubt a general acceptance of those clear moral principles which can then be taught with confidence in the schools and will then be upheld in the nation at large by all the instruments of publicity, by all persons of influence and especially by the common sense of a strong public opinion. Can there be found any such clear moral principles? Not if dictated as a universal moral code claiming universal acceptance. Morality cannot be taught as a code. It can only be taught effectively by personal examples, and through the words and actions of teachers in every kind of trade or occupation who do not confuse generosity of spirit with general permissiveness nor obedience with servility nor individual enterprise with licence to do whatever attracts.

It has been the custom in this country to give this teaching through the Bible. The great advantage of this is that the text book is in the hands of everyone; that all the evil and covetous desires of mankind and all their frustrations are splendidly illustrated in stories of real people taken from real life; that the Old Testament begins with a splendid folk story of man's disobedience and goes on to set out in the Ten Commandments the means by which Moses tried to educate an ill-disciplined and grumbling lot of tribesmen in principles of community good order; that the Old Testament as a whole sets out the general failure, even of a chosen people, to respond to God made known to them in a code of command, disobedience, punishment, sacrifice and forgiveness; while in the New Testament is related the history of Jesus Christ and of his first followers and of their teaching of the good life which still stands out as the best source of enlightened consideration of social morality. For the New Testament sets before men not a code but an aspiration and a faith to live by and aspire to.

Whether they know how to use the Bible or not, heads of families and all adult citizens can only discharge their duty to the community if they are honouring the same moral principles which the schools are trying to teach to the adolescents. In other words the adult must have the grace to believe that morally at least he is only an adolescent himself. On this foundation alone can men claim to possess rights in or against society or nations claim rights for themselves. Apart from some such a foundation as this, no declaration of human rights can have any popular sanction. The Church must not presume to dictate in this matter: but it is its duty to give wise advice to the State about it, and advice which can claim to represent in some measure the *consensus fidelium* in the Church.

36

Discussion

PEOPLE learn whether in school or elsewhere by discussion and personal application, not by dictation. If the child is to learn how to regulate and turn to good use his individual desires and actions, it must be by discussion with other people, some of whom are wiser than he is, related to his own experiences and actions. All general issues affecting our society in some notable way become the subject of general discussion both in the daily small talk of the community and in the various organs of publicity. Such discussion provides the life blood of a free community and the only way by which public opinion can be kept lively and healthy. Nevertheless no citizen who takes an intelligent part in this perpetual discourse by ear, eye or mouth can profit by it unless he has enough of a critical faculty to enable him to distinguish between truth and fiction, wisdom and unwisdom, the balanced and the biased, and at the end of the discussion to know whether he is in a position to commit himself to a conclusion or would be wiser to suspend judgement or to do no more than adopt a provisional view or non-view of the matter under discussion.

It is unfortunately true that much of the endless torrent of discussion of topics of general interest, moral or political, to which we are exposed in the modern world is almost valueless. Too much of it is spent in passing on idle gossip, or in retailing what is no more than rumour, or in assigning motives to persons for their public actions which can be no more than guesswork and often enough of malicious guesswork. Passing judgement on other people is always a perilous thing to do since inevitably at the same time the speaker is passing judgement on himself and his own merits or deficiencies, whether he speaks as a private person, or from a pulpit, in the public house or in print.

A discussion to be profitable to all taking part in it calls for three things. It needs contributors to it who know the facts of the matter reasonably well or at least well enough to avoid and to correct mis-statements of fact likely to lead the discussion into errors of judgement. It is my experience that if a person has the necessary knowledge and ventures to correct a mis-statement, it more often than not provokes contradiction, unless he has already established a reputation as a reliable witness and unless with his knowledge he has learned how to contribute it in a wise and helpful manner. It needs a common recognition among those taking part that there are conventions of reasonable thinking by which experiences must be controlled and arguments disciplined. And thirdly the accepted purpose of the discussion must be the advancement of understanding, a constructive and not a destructive end, a raising and not a lowering of the moral outlook on the affairs of the community—in fact the achieving of wisdom and the training of ourselves to be wise men to the best of our abilities. And for many people the height of their wisdom will be to say little but to see which of the sharers in the discussion wins their trust as faithful men and good citizens.[1]

In fact every discussion of such issues ought to be only a continuation class of the spirit of school education. There the teacher is the accepted authority. He or she knows the facts of the subject matter, has been trained to contribute them in a wise and helpful manner, has been trained in all the arts and skills of imaginative reasonable thinking, is professionally committed to a constructive purpose in relation to all the pupils in his or her charge; and he is in the wrong vocation unless possessed all the time of a pastoral sense which expresses itself in a moral sympathy and service, and unless he is a humble teacher of wisdom and an exemplar of it. Of course every teacher fails in many ways: but every teacher tries as best he or she can; and most of them bring to their pupils not only a real devotion to them together with a keen interest in what they teach, but also some living touch of inspiration which abides in their pupils and bears fruit.

In the school environment the teacher has authority, is listened to and obeyed: otherwise there is disorder, and everyone's talents are being wasted or misdirected to futile excursions into provocation, prevarication, and punishment. Far and away the most dangerous and destructive feature of modern society is the breakdown of the concept of authority as having a moral claim to obedience, not of course an absolute or an unreasonable claim, but a moral claim: and reason, wisdom, knowledge all have a necessary part to play in keeping the citizen to the path of duty and of moral integrity.

[1] It is a fact that perhaps most people do not seek to be guided by reason in public affairs. They enjoy every appeal to emotion. When in doubt they tend to go with their own crowd. Publicists, religious and secular, are always liable to exploit this situation unfairly.

In the floods of public discussion of the sort we are considering there is no recognised authority present able to claim a moral authority of this sort. There is in fact a vacuum at this point.[1] Each person present must be conscious of the duty of providing his own best contribution of wisdom which has its own moral authority: and in every discussion it is of the utmost importance that there should be made evident the word of wisdom and wise moral direction by those present who have wisdom. Those who have only contributed false witness or aggressive individualisms should not be left to feel that they had achieved anything useful by their self-willed resistance to the voice of wisdom.

[1] Except for the discipline of the subject matter to which I referred earlier. That authority cannot be altered or avoided. But men in their follies and false enthusiasms can fail to pay due respect to it and leave later generations to reap the evil consequences of so doing. This is the truth which the Mosaic code was trying to express when it said 'I the Lord thy God am a jealous God and visit the sins of the fathers upon the children . . .'.

37

Discourtesy

It is worth while to pause over this word discourtesy for a few moments. A discourteous person is an *uncivil* and so an *uncivilised* person. An illmannered person disturbs the harmony of a society in an ungenerous and unintelligent manner. It is not discourteous at all to state one's own opinion frankly and firmly in any society or to take one's own line where it is relevant and graciously done. Humour and the sharpness of wit with its slight tinge of malice has a place and a spice of its own so long as it is not devoid of grace. But when a member of any society is bad mannered and deliberately introduces a discordant note out of folly or out of malice or out of the itch to assert himself or show himself off, then his discourtesy is rightly to be described as uncivilised. That is what it is to 'behave oneself unseemly'. And such behaviour raises inevitably a moral issue—was such behaviour necessary, wise, Christian?

A simple example of this dilemma on a small scale is presented by the issue of bad language in conversation or of obscenity in literature. I do not know any kind of civilised society in which it is not discourteous to use language which is generally regarded as 'bad'. A television programme a short while ago included a forceful character who hardly uttered a sentence which did not include a stream of 'bloodys'. There is nothing wrong with the word in any technical sense: it is not intrinsically wrong. But neither is it a colourless word nor one accepted as an ornamental word for general use in ordinary homes. In

the programme referred to, projected into a vast number
of ordinary homes, this multiplicity of 'bloodys' obtruding
itself as a special feature of the item was, as it seemed to
me, unnecessary from any point of view, terribly tedious
to listen to and thoroughly inartistic. A B.B.C. producer
ought in my judgement to have had the sense and the wit
to avoid such an effect—fundamentally because it was a
piece of discourtesy to impose it on society in general.

The same and a good deal more may be said about
'four-letter words'. Writing as I am on an Australian visit,
I take the following news item from an Australian daily
paper. I do not know what the particular words are or
mean: but this kind of dispute is as common in England
as in Australia.

> The Queensland Premier at the weekend stepped into the
> dispute over the words '. . . boongs' in a Brisbane produced
> play when he announced that future use of similar words on
> stage would be investigated.

The newspaper went on to say that a report on the use
of such words, which were obscene by law in theatre pro-
ductions would be made in due course by the Minister of
Justice.

It is generally recognised that there must be some laws
prohibiting and punishing obscenity in order to protect
society from having its general sense of decency outraged
and debased. At the same time it is foolish to expect that
the law can decide at what point a word or a scene in a
book or a play becomes obscenity of such a kind that it
must be regarded as illegal. Under British law, thanks
very largely to the genial and entertaining endeavours of
A. P. Herbert, what many people might regard as obscene
may become lawful if experts judge that its excellence as
literature and as a work of imagination excuses its possible

obscenity. There can be no end to the argument, except to abolish control by law which leaves society at the mercy of those whose trade it is to dramatise the evil and obscene in the hearts of men.

All these obscenities and four-letter words are related in some way to the physical reactions of men and women; and the use of them may therefore awake or encourage physical desires and are to be regarded as 'erotic'. But this word needs care. It comes from the Greek word meaning love as desire and includes all that stimulates physical desire. It must be sharply distinguished from another word *Agape*, which also means love, but non-passionate love, non-erotic love, non-physical love, purely spiritual love. I doubt whether, man being the creature he is, it is at all possible to distinguish absolutely between spiritual love and animal love, spiritual desire and physical desire; but in some people and at some times spiritual desire has really extinguished all physical desire, and in some people and at some times physical desire entirely extinguishes all spiritual desire. There can be no doubt that in general whether in conversation or in literature the word love is used with a predominant reference to physical desire and its satisfaction. There can be no doubt at all that of these two meanings spiritual love is the higher, the better, the nobler, the more imaginative—in fact more akin to the eternal and to the love of God for us: for God's love though essentially a love of desire reaching out to us, is essentially also a spiritual love free from any physical conditioning. Of these two, animal love is the lower, the less noble, the more transient, perishable, passing. All obscenities are obscene because they appeal unreasonably to the physical as opposed to the spiritual part of a human being's make up. It may be thought that the appeal is made so artistically that the spiritual loss will at least in artistic people be negligible and the literary concentration on the physical desire harmless. If that be so, all the more is a true discrimination beyond the reach of the Law. All the arguments in cases like that of *Lady Chatterley's Lover* are really about imponderables. One can only say that some of them are out of place, that the publicity causes many to read the book for the wrong motive, and that such cases spring partly from some publisher's estimate of whether he can profitably publish the book. *De gustibus non disputandum.* In such matters the law is always at a disadvantage.

But of course there is another possibility—not to write or publish the possible obscenity, not to speak the objectionable four-letter word. And it is at this point that the moral issue lies and the moral judgement must be made by the writer or the speaker or the publisher: and the moral issue is very largely (at least *prima facie*) a question between courtesy and discourtesy, between civil behaviour or uncivilised behaviour.[1] As always, everything ends up as a matter of personal decision and personal action or inaction (whether chosen or enforced upon one). This applies to bad or disturbing use of language in public just as much as to any other moral issue. Because desire is so dangerous and often so devilish an element in everyone's life, there is in this field less room than in many others for unthinking folly, for malice, for aggressiveness, for exhibitionism or any other form of irresponsibility.

I must not pursue this topic of discourtesy into other fields: but this much I must say. The politician who falls

[1] It must be recognised that some people regard it as their duty (and it may come to be seen as a very welcome duty) to take some form of behaviour regarded as uncivilised and to civilise it or at least to turn it to some good use. I do not try to deal with them here. There is need for a treatise on the ethics of remonstrance, rebellion, and reconciliation.

into gross discourtesy or abusive denunciation of his opponents or just into abuse of them, deserves to be regarded as doing great damage to his own reputation and great harm both to his cause and to the public interest. This is specially true of those who speak in Parliament. It is there very easy to get a reputation for speeches of little substance but much abuse, for what outside the protected walls of Parliament would be regarded as rude, irresponsible and discourteous speech. It is noticeable what deep respect is won in Parliament and elsewhere by those men and women who, speaking with reasonable knowledge and skill, never indulge in empty discourtesies.[1]

The Press is often involved in protecting the freedom of the Press as though it were a sacred institution, above criticism. If there is blame to be found in any particular instance, it must be looked for in the personal discretion and moral sensitiveness of the editors with whom all responsibility ultimately rests. But none of us can penetrate into their secrets: and how wise is the injunction 'Judge not that ye be not judged.' Courtesy should be quick to say 'I am sorry' and editors in their public capacity cannot often say that even if they feel it. But they must never cease to be judging *themselves* honestly. Courtesy is only a part of loving our neighbours as we love ourselves.

[1] It is distressing to see how often reporters and interviewers seem to press their enquiries far beyond the limits of courtesy, whether they are speaking to public persons on public issues or to private individuals caught up in some happening, often one bringing to them deep personal sorrow.

38

Disputes and Strife

WE are surrounded on all sides by disputes—economic, trade, legal, cultural, theological disputes and all the rest. It will be sufficient if in this study of Christians in the world we confine ourselves to political disputes and strife.

We may note first that almost every newspaper almost always reports political news in terms of conflict and too often assists in stoking up the fires of political passion and strife. Most politicians do the same. It is queer that while some psychologists tell us that children should not be encouraged to play with guns and weapons of war, and any parent knows better than to let children play with fire, so many so-called adults in the realm of politics (and politics includes every issue involving public order) delight in putting weapons of political warfare into the hands of those less informed than they are themselves, and in teaching and training them to play with fire and to become political incendiaries. There we are. What is there that the good citizen and the good Christian can do about it?

First and most important, he must try to get a general idea of what the dispute is about or, since that is often quite impossible for the plain citizen, of what it has started from: and that may well mean getting clear who put the match to this particular blaze. Thus, if I may venture to particularise, the match which started the blaze about Rhodesia was Mr. Ian Smith's declaration of independence of Rhodesia from the British Crown: and it will be remembered that he put the match to the fire in spite of earnest appeals made jointly by Mr. Wilson as Prime Minister and by Sir Alec Douglas Home, his predecessor as Prime Minister, not to do this thing. Partisans should never be allowed to obscure that initial fact by overlaying it with other aspects of the dispute. In the same way nothing should be allowed to obscure the fact that the British Crown inherited a direct responsibility to protect the interests of all citizens of Rhodesia whatever their colour, and is right not to surrender that responsibility until assured that it will still be scrupulously and generously discharged and constitutionally secured. If that starting point is honestly accepted, the dispute can remain a reasonable search for a constructive agreement. But if one or both parties to this or any other dispute fail to accept a common starting point of agreement, then nothing can limit or end the dispute except (at immense cost spiritual and economic to all concerned) efflux of time together with surrender by one side or the other or (even worse) a face-saving compromise lacking the clean and wholesome lines of an honest surrender. Behind all such disputes is the catastrophe of the fixed idea. Anyone who is governed by a fixed idea, whether churchman or plain citizen, is an idealist of a sort who has surrendered to an ideology of some sort. He thinks that his idea has some kind of absolute value which he must not betray, and lacks the wisdom to discipline his idea in the light of experience, observation and common sense. The obstinacy of an idealist is incapable of co-operation or generosity. This is true of those who commit themselves to any ideology whether it be capitalism, communism, catholicism or any other 'ism', all of which indicate some kind of closed system of thought. In my last few days in Australia I saw certain proposals for laws to control strikes described from the side of the employers as 'utterly ineffective' and from the trade union side as a tyrannical assault on the freedom of the worker; while here in an Australian paper I have just read that:

> The major problem with the collective bargaining system was that if negotiations broke down a test of strength between the two sides took place because of the lack of third party intervention.

The writer, speaking for Australian trade unions, was maintaining that the arbitration system is still the best for Australia. But the next day I read in the same paper that the secretary of the Australian Council of Salaried and Professional Associations had said that:

> Employers were too prone to use arbitration courts instead of conciliation as a means of settling industrial disputes. The worker was forced reluctantly and often too quickly to take his claims to arbitration. In the arbitration courts legal attitudes tended to predominate before the practical and moral issues involved in a claim saw the light of day.

There is the perennial problem in England as in Australia—how to bring to an end, and even more to a healing and reconciling end, disputes which are destroying the harmonious working and the economic stability of the nation. By some form of conciliation which is a restoration of co-operation? Of course that is the right way. But if conciliation is foiled by obstinacy on one side or the other or both, what then? By compulsory arbitration? But as the passage just quoted shows, it may be misused and workers may have a reason or an excuse for thinking that it is being used to their disadvantage. What then? There must be a final voice to replace endless strife; and it is inevitable in a civilised community to say that the law must decide. And at once everyone is suspicious, for the reason given above that before the law legal attitudes and precedents tend to predominate and the moral issues involved in a claim cannot be examined or assessed: and while the Government is chiefly concerned with the practical ending of a ruinous dispute, the citizen, without the knowledge or ability to adjudicate on the particular issue, is compelled to take sides on what he supposes the moral issues to be as seen through a glass darkly. And how is the worker involved in the dispute and involved emotionally and economically in it, torn by conflicting loyalties, to form a right judgement about it?

One thing can be said at once. In earlier days strikes, official and unofficial, were the only weapons the manual workers had with which to fight the grievous evils of oppression and poverty from which they suffered, and to win relief from them. They were the last weapons left in the hands of those suffering desperately from the last straw. Strikes today are utterly unlike those of earlier days. Official strikes occur in a long battle of power between the two most powerful sections of the community; those with the capital and those with the labour with which to serve one another. Unofficial strikes occur chiefly from impatience, irritation and lack of a controlled sense of responsibility: but there is no place for them at all in a civilised community where it is recognised that from top to bottom we are all tied to one another in bonds of mutual responsibility, and in which all are free to speak their minds responsibly and forcibly, free to disagree and no less free to agree in any dispute. What then? Disputes and strifes are little due to the particular issue declared to be at stake: they are due far more to inherited attitudes and prejudices and preconceived opinions and personal dislikes and spiritual indigestions and spiritual traumas and lack of imagination and density of skin and all the rest of the ills which displace generosity of spirit and wise understanding from the lives of men.

Deliverance can come only as disputants can learn to forget prejudices, to give their minds to the relevant issues, to think dispassionately and to seek a wise and peaceful outcome—or, I might more hopefully say, as disputants can learn to do what the wisest among them advise them to do. Very often the Christian will be specially helpful in discovering the way from strife to fellowship; but let me add at once, not always. For Christians are not always well-informed or wise, and some are as foolish and head-strong as any can be.

Wise Christians and wise citizens and those who are both will try to be patient, long-suffering, both grumbling and cheerful, peaceable and generous in spirit while the militants fight it out and wise men will seek to provide an authority able to end a dispute by speaking a last word which all will accept as the last word, at least for the time being while the healing processes of nature and of grace do their godly work.

The Christian will pay special heed to words from the epistle of St. James:

> Let every man be quick to hear, slow to speak, slow to anger; for the anger of man does not work the righteousness of God . . . For if anyone is a hearer of the word and not a doer he is like a man who observes his natural face in a mirror; for he observes himself and goes away and at once forgets what he looks like. But he who looks into the perfect law, the law of freedom and is no hearer who forgets but a doer that acts (according to that perfect law) he shall be blessed in his deed.

And the Christian remembers too that to serve Christ *is* perfect freedom.

39

Violence

I WANT first to make a distinction between *force* and *violence*. They both mean strength, but strength differently used. Perhaps we may differentiate somehow like this. In every society from a family to the nation there is a proper place for force. In the family or the school a smack in time may save nine. Every nation must have its police force and (as things are) its fighting forces. It is to be assumed that generally speaking force of this kind will be used with discretion, under wise control and to constructive ends. On the other hand violence carries with it the idea of force used without discretion, out of control, impetuous, unrestrained, destructive. The use of violence violates the good order and good sense of the community. The grim thing is that since it can only be restrained effectively by counter force, it creates the conditions of warfare in which the users of violence may not recognise any rules of warfare or indeed of common decency.

Here I shall only consider, and that briefly, the violent temper which inclines a person to be violent. It is always uncivilised conduct when any person gives in to a violent temper. It is to some extent evil behaviour and anti-social behaviour in a person whether the weapon he uses is physical or verbal, a violence of action or a violence of language and speech, because he has to some extent lost control of himself. The present wave of student violence in this country is particularly regrettable, because this country has for so many centuries been trying to train students above all in the self-control necessary to the acquisition of graces with which to benefit and serve the common good.[1] In these testing days students should be among the first to understand that the citizen's first duty is to acquire by self-control and self-discipline the true values of an educated mind with which to pay their own way through life and make their best contribution to the life of the community.

It may be said that where people resort to violence, it is always the result of provocation. But that is not so. There are some who seem to be born to violence of speech and action as the sparks fly upward. There are others who can point to the causes which provoke them to violence, which however very often when examined are seen to call for quite different responses. Almost always the violent outburst is due either to a kind of greed (the lust for power or self-importance), to fear (of losing some element of self-respect or self-interest) or to rebellion against authority.

All who begin an open demonstration of rebellion or remonstrance, however in itself well-intentioned and well-directed, must reckon with the fact that it will be likely in the end as it grows in size to become a centre of violence, and of unjustifiable provocation to peaceable citizens.

The constructive purpose of a demonstration is to draw attention to an evil or an injustice which calls for remedy. But if it wins no publicity for itself, it produces no effect. It tends therefore to seek more attention, which means more publicity. But the merits of a demonstration cannot be judged by the amount of publicity it gains; the larger the size of the demonstration and the publicity it wins, the more

[1] William Temple used to say that the great distinction of the English system of education, at least at the universities, was that students lived together in a common life. Thus they learned together to acquire knowledge and to acquire the arts of living together in fellowship.

liable it is to degenerate into a mood of violence and the less does it become amenable to reasonable or civil control. Even if it achieves a practical purpose of some kind, it has done so by force; and has not created the good-will which is necessary for any real advance in unity of civic harmony: it has very likely merely whetted the appetite for more provocative demonstration and for lawless (even though not unlawful) demands. But an ordered society can only be a generous and a stable society where truth is respected and authority upheld by trust between all its members.

In this country the disturbing thing is that too many groups and interests are at one and the same time seeking publicity for their own grievances and demanding under threats some reform which will give more power to the less responsible and less respect to the more responsible. The result is to encourage unduly those inclined to a militant temper, who are already too much encouraged by the current militancy of speech and ambition among all the nations and its exaggeration day by day by all the organs of publicity, printed and visual.

As always the problem is that of the restraints of personal responsibility holding their own place against the forces of disorderly demonstration. Law can do something among a law abiding people: but it is only by an inbred sense of restraint, patience, good humour and trust of one another overruling the dangerously foolish, hastily reformist, headily idealist, attractions to violence that a society can grow, as it should, wisely and fruitfully from one period of maturity to another. The Christian will know that at the root of all health in society is the divine injunction which conjoins 'Thou shalt love thy neighbour as thyself' with 'Thou shalt love the Lord thy God' in a common allegiance.

40

Politics, Home and Abroad

THERE are no longer any purely domestic politics. What happens in one small corner of a country may be reported in every corner of the world, and in the reporting may be inflated, distorted, degraded by organs of publicity. An upset in one country's domestic economy may affect the value of money in homes and offices all over the world. The Christian and the citizen have the same duty and the same interest, to keep their heads, and to encourage in themselves and others a quiet spirit which seeks to think and act soberly, advisedly, discreetly, reverently and in the fear of God. To that end I contribute here what I can from my own experience.

All political problems, however tense or tragic must be controlled, lived through, and solved so far as a solution is obtainable, by the nation or nations directly concerned in them The responsibility is on them. No outside nation has any natural right to interfere except by giving constructive advice. No outside body of opinion has any right to do or say anything to aggravate the problem or to foment the conflict. Even well-intentioned interference is fraught with danger and is likely to embitter and prolong the conflict. Advice from outside organs of publicity must be discreet, wise, humbly given and plainly more constructive than critical. Only where this advice is followed by writers and speakers, by newspapers and leader writers, by men and women in the street and in the home is there any hope that those responsible for handling the problem, conducting the negotiations, controlling the results will be able to bring right and righteous minds to bear on the problem. Perhaps the chief sinners against settlements of any sort are those who write and publish articles retailing indiscriminately (or still worse, with a 'slant') all that they have heard or can guess about the attitudes or activities of the men and women carrying the chief responsibility, about their personal characters and their relations with their opponents or with one another. The effect is to make everyone angry or envious. Every political and international problem which does not remain in a state of 'cold war' must end in some kind of co-operative solution, one to which all sides give their consent even if some of them consent only by accepting defeat of their own purposes. No critic from outside the struggle, no gossip in any country, has a right to speak at all unless his purpose is to prepare or point the way to a co-operative issue: and that requires the introduction into the issue of some whispers of generosity of spirit, some faint suggestions of a tolerable outcome; never mere denunciation or despair. The leader in some national conflict of interests at home who says that there is no alternative but to fight is certainly looking in the wrong direction. I remember that in a dreadfully dangerous and damaging national strike a few years ago the general secretary of the union on strike said that of course if they were thinking of the country there would be no strike, but, he added, charity begins at home. Our country is our home and it is here that charity has first to do its redeeming work. When any issue goes sour and bitter (and how many today *start* like that), the leaders of it should kneel and pray to whatever God outside or inside themselves they acknowledge that some measure of generosity of spirit may be granted them, that so they may not miss any opportunity of serving their country and the whole body of their fellow citizens in an hour of need. The good of the country must govern all political action and must be seen to govern it. For international problems, there is a golden rule. No nation in the world is entitled to use force against another independent nation, whether it is by an open declaration of war or otherwise unless first it has reported the *casus belli* to the United Nations and has listened to its advice. The charter allows a loophole in that in the event of a sudden crisis a nation may have to act first and report afterwards. I have never been more ashamed than when I heard the defenders of our action over Suez trying in the House of Lords to excuse their refusal to take the matter to the United Nations. But of course it will be said that the United Nations is of no practical use. There is of course a lot of truth in it, but that is only because all men are so inefficient at overcoming their own selfish pursuits of power, and men entrenched in their national isolations less efficient still. The United Nations Organisation is an attempt to rescue nations from their supposed self-sufficiencies! It is the permanent evidence that hope is invincible.

The most dangerous argument that can be used in relation to conflicts within or between nations is also the most generous one—the desire, the longing to help the weak, to heal the wounded, to stop some misery and suffering and injustice, to avenge the wrongs. Here I must state very clearly my own view, knowing well that many citizens and many Christians will wish to differ from me. I am convinced that sympathy of this sort is not enough to justify a nation in taking action within the jurisdiction of another nation against its will. To give a concrete example, the British Government has made its attitude to the

Vietnam war entirely clear and has expressed its fears and beliefs. In so doing it has fulfilled its duty to the United States, and to the whole family of nations. Those in this country who have been making violent attacks upon the policies of the United States in this respect are showing an unseemly concern with what is not within their province of responsibility or that of our Government. Citizens of this country are of course free to demonstrate peacefully against the Vietnam war; but even there, as it seems to me, they must respect the decencies of human relationships. They must show a proper regard for the Government of another country as it meets a responsibility and a duty to which it has become committed, a duty now entirely unwelcome but from which there is at present no obvious way of escape. It would be easy to give other examples where demonstrations become improper and harmful and where criticism of another nation is only wise if clearly made in a constructive spirit.[1]

In our own domestic problems also the place for sympathy is to be noted. In the last century the poor, the under-privileged, the unjustly treated could not make themselves heard: those who 'had' were mostly unaware of and insensitive to the lot of those who 'had not'. Issues had to be fought out in terms of human suffering. But in the Britain of today, the situation is quite different. Where there is injustice and under-privilege, there are certain to be advocates of reform at work, doing what is best begun by voluntary effort and enthusiasm. There will of course be frustrating difficulties in getting the ear of the public, in getting plans for betterment considered, in getting

---

[1] It is to be noted that in the recent civil war in Nigeria, the chief British agencies for sending relief to the starving multitudes in 'Biafra' were scrupulously careful (as was the British Government) to respect the authority of the Government of Nigeria.

legislation if that is what is needed. But the light will be shining and the darkness will not prevail over it for ever; and there is a proper place in this tortured world for long-suffering. But today most of the disputes are caused by a combination of desire for more money and desire for more prestige, and are economically damaging and destructive to all the members of the community with no counter-vailing advantages. Where sympathy might wish to operate, it is strangled by the fact that the grievance is ventilated and exploited by organised bodies concerned to promote their own political or economic ends to the utmost. Because the points at issue are highly complicated and technical the general public cannot judge their merits; though there is not likely now to be any general sympathy with any who turn an industrial issue into a display of obstinate militancy. It is not yet seen to be the duty of all with responsibility of any sort to use all their endeavours to restrain the militants, to abolish causes of strife, to encourage the spirit of co-operation and mutual trust in all walks of life throughout the country. Without that the country will not be a happy community, and it will not even be able to pay its way in the world. We are by nature a generous and a humorous people. The damage is done by those in public life who lack generosity of spirit which means that they also lack the power of laughing at them-selves and so are unable to help us to laugh with one another, without malice and without offence.

There is one other aspect of this matter which I think I must mention though I will do so as briefly as I can. What about the Church in politics?

The Christian is as free as any other citizen to have a view about political or sociological or international matters. He has also just as much right as any other citizen, not to bother his head about them too much, but to leave others, Christians and citizens together, with more time and ability for that kind of thing than he has to look after them. From time to time some leader like William Temple or some cause like Biafra will engage his special interest, and he will bring all that he has learned from Christ through the gospels and from the Holy Spirit through his daily behaviour to bear upon these questions. But he will never suppose that he is competent to commit himself to supporting political decisions or to espousing some political cause just because his interest has been specially aroused or his sympathies vividly awakened. Jesus Christ said a great deal about sociology, about how to meet the experiences of daily life in prosperity and in adversity, about how to meet them in the spirit of the kingdom of God. There are two incidents from his life which it is right and relevant to recall here. When he was asked a political question about taxation by the authorities, he refused to answer except by saying that we must always face the task of distinguishing between the claims of society and the claims of God and do our best to do our duty to both. When he was told that Roman soldiers had massacred some Galileans as they were offering sacrifices to God so that their blood and the blood of their sacrifices intermingled, he thought it wise to say no more than that so long as men in general act after the spirit of those soldiers, we shall all be in danger of such destruction; it is as though he said—'Repent together or perish together; seek the kingdom of God or end your days in the kingdom of men.'

The Christians who feel as many most rightly feel that they are called to be active in secular politics (or, for that matter, in Church politics) must obey with special care such restraining cautions as I have mentioned above as applying to all citizens; and such a one will be careful to remember that while his service to Christ governs all that he says or thinks, it does not necessarily give him any more talents than, or as many talents as, belong to his neighbours, Christian or non-Christian. It is his duty to use only the talents he has been entrusted with, to use them humbly and constructively, and at all times to seek reconciliation and peace.[1]

A word must be said of those who speak for the Church to the world, whether World Council of Churches or British Council of Churches or Church Assemblies or Bishops or Popes. None of them must ever presume to dictate to governments or secular authorities. Christ did not equip them for such work, and as St. Paul said, these authorities exist in the providence of God, and have to bear their own burdens of responsibilities. No Church body or churchman can relieve them of that responsibility or share it with them. Without it no one is in a position of final authority in a secular state. All a Church body can do is to deliver its own opinion, make if necessary its own protests and to seek opportunity to give good and helpful advice. But as always there is a time to speak and a time to keep silence. And when something ought to be said by or for the Church, it must be said humbly without presumption, and helpfully by way of pointing in the direction which might lead to good order and healthy peace. Mere pious affirmations may do harm. Church bodies must never forget how fond they have often shown themselves to be of giving advice from inadequate knowledge

---

[1] The Church is called to be the Church Militant. Every Christian must have an element of militancy in him, by which to fight against 'sin, the world and the devil' (cf. the Baptism service): but it is a spiritual warfare even when its weapons are not entirely spiritual.

and without wise understanding. Job's response to his advisers must not be forgotten: No doubt you are the people and wisdom will die with you! But I have understanding as well as you; I am not inferior to you.

But yet more, while Church bodies have no right to do more than give the best advice they can to secular authorities (and of course to suffer at their hands) only very rarely can they have the right to commit or seem to commit all Christians to a particular course of political action. Their word to them can rarely be more than a word of strong advice. The British Council of Churches often receives reports from its committees on current issues demanding the most anxious consideration by churchmen of all Churches, racialism, Rhodesia, Nigeria, sex, abortion, and the like. These reports, as I have seen over the years, are very carefully prepared by very able persons with great experience. They are invaluable: but never are they the last word. Sometimes they look like attempting to tell the Government or the nation or Christians in general what ought to be done. But every Christian has the right and duty to judge for himself or herself. It is quite certain that no report of this kind will ever command universal consent: it is certain that on any matters of importance there will be real and possibly acute differences of opinion. The bigger the council, the less can it say by way of practical advice, the more it is bound to take refuge in generalities; and all it can do with them is to commend them to the consideration of the autonomous Churches. These councils of today, like those of earlier days in the life of the Church, have no real authority of their own. Each particular Church is its own ultimate authority under God. I am satisfied that these councils as such should never do more than *receive* a report (which is a non-committal act) on matters of current politics, and *commend* it to the attention of the Churches represented on the council and to Christian people generally. Councils will also on occasion very rightly commend a report to the attention of the public generally and to governments in particular.

Thus and in all other ways Christians and Churches may rightly claim respectful attention for the opinions they offer on politics or any other moral problem. Such attention they have a right to demand. They have no right to command agreement. It is thus that governments and people in general come to respect and value at their true worth the opinions of Christians and churchmen thus responsibly presented.

41

For Example

I refer in these concluding chapters to three particular problems which are acutely relevant today, as sociological and as moral problems and therefore as problems for Christians. It would not be relevant to my general purpose to discuss any of them at length: but a great deal of importance can be said about them in a short compass. The three problems may be called Money, Sex, Work: but I want to refer only to Money Control, Sex Control, and Attitude to Work; and to deal with these as personal problems only, which everyone must meet as best he can: and what he makes of life here will depend very largely upon the spirit in which he meets them.

I will introduce what I have to say by recalling an incident from the long conversation lasting well over an hour which I had in December, 1960, with Pope John XXIII. Just now I referred to the virtue of generosity of spirit. There has never been a better or more potent example of generosity of spirit than was to be seen in Pope John XXIII. With him I should wish to bracket Archbishop William Temple, of whom I said on the tablet to his memory in Repton School Chapel, *Amoris Dei exemplar et interpres*. Both of these eminently simple and eminently gifted men were indeed examples of the love of God and interpreters of it to their fellow men.

In my conversation with Pope John, which was mainly about our common interests in leading a Christian life, the Pope quoted Thomas-à-Kempis to the effect that for a Christian if there was a choice between *more* or *less*, the answer was generally *less*: and I recalled to him that in the New Testament the Greek word for covetousness was *wanting more*,[1] and is closely linked with idolatry. As will be seen in relation to money and sex, the choice is generally just between *more* or *less* than is proper: while as to work the problem is to find the right way of measuring and valuing it.

Perhaps here I might relate another incident from my conversation with Pope John. He had quoted to me a passage from a recent address of his in which as it happened occurred a reference to the time when his 'separated brethren' would return to the Church of Rome. I said, 'Your Holiness, not *return*.' Surprised by this, he asked me to explain, to which I said: 'None of us can go backwards, only forwards. Our two Churches are advancing on

[1] The Greek word is *pleonexia*. See St. Paul to the Colossians, 3:5 'Covetousness which is idolatry'.

parallel courses and we may look forward to their meeting one day.' After a pause, he said, 'You are quite right' and I never heard him again speak of our 'returning'. That incident is not irrelevant to these chapters. It is by such easy conversation between people who trust each other that fixed ideas from the past get unfrozen and liquidated. Thus we can learn to travel together by learning from the past and at the same time unlearning what needs to be unlearned, by looking forward to the future without being deceived by our own ideas of what forms fulfilment should take; and so by humility and intelligence ordering our steps sensibly in the present.

42

Control of Money

No one can tell us what money really is. It is no longer gold. It is a means of exchange, but it also has moods of its own, and men whose business it is to work in the money market are unable to control its moods or predict its movements. In the end (and often at the beginning too) the value of money is a matter of trust, mistrust and speculation. No wonder it is the least stable, the most volatile of all the factors of modern life. There are wise economists and wise financiers and wise sociologists who try to advise the nation as to how its economy can be better managed. Governments do their best to keep earning and spending at home and overseas in a healthy relation; and since it affects each man's pocket a Government has to act under a constant fire of criticism, informed and uninformed, obstruction and active opposition all of which is ostensibly in the interests of the country and its business but is deeply affected also by private interests and organised prejudices. It is almost impossible to come across a truly balanced summary of the situation economically and yet more impossible to find it related in a truly balanced manner to the political situation. The British people have a well deserved reputation for shrewdness of judgement and also for defending themselves against short-sighted enthusiasms or alarms: but history has plenty of examples of their failure in both respects and of their surrender to short-sighted selfishness. Christians and other citizens of special experience or insight do an immense service to us all by helping the nation to understand where they are and where they are going, and especially by enlightening and enlivening the consciences of our people—so that there may be some conscious and purposeful effort in action among us to reject the evil and to choose the good in the economy of the nation.

But each one of us has his and her own personal problems in so far as choice or decision exist for the individual and are under the control of personal will. We must earn our living and pay our way by what we are and by what we do, by our own character and skill. Apart from what we must spend in order to maintain a decent standard of living appropriate to our surroundings, we have the power to settle for ourselves, more or less freely, the general scale and manner of our 'spending' within the limits of our 'getting'. In spirit we must be generous but not lavish, saving but not stingy. Thus we shall make our way through life wrestling with money just as we wrestle with any other of our moral problems. But there are two special problems which must be noted.

In a general way it is not good to live on borrowed money even for a short time. For this there is a simple and sufficient reason. If we borrow money we are committed to pay interest on it and to pay it back: but we cannot control the future nor say for certain that we will be able to go on paying the interest till we have paid back the debt. Thus in fact by borrowing, we lose control of ourselves. St. Paul was right: 'owe no man anything, except to love one another'. There is nothing wrong in money itself or in charging interest on money lent: both are sensible and useful tools. Nor is it wrong to borrow with a promise to repay: but for an individual it is always liable to be or become dangerous. The hire purchase system is obviously very helpful to many people at a particular time for a particular purpose: but it has very great dangers: it can be abused as a habit; and many people abuse it by committing themselves to repayments which are really beyond their means or are disproportionate to their other spending. And since habits are powerful things in our lives, it is a serious moral complication when a family or a person departs from the simple moral precept of spending only what one has available to spend. It is to lose some element of self-control and commit oneself to some extent to the vagaries of fortune and to luck.

And luck creates another special problem. Our response to life should be a reasonable one. Life is already certain to bring us many hazards, moral, physical, spiritual, personal, domestic, national. We shall not be able to meet them unless we have trained ourselves to stand up to them, to take them as they come, to meet them with courage, with reason, and with faith. It is stupid to introduce into our lives another hazard, to get dependent even for our amusement on the element of luck, to build luck into our lives at all. In relation to money above all, because it is specially liable to be turned to evil or self-indulgent or self-destructive uses, we should be careful not to weaken our own powers of self-control and self-management.

It is a fact that all round us are ceaseless invitations to entrust ourselves to luck and that most forms of business are built up on the principle of borrowing money to finance them. Such borrowing is a regular and a respectable part of the national economy. Yet even that is not without great dangers; it easily comes to make inroads on the integrity of some: it opens the door to private interests which may prefer the private to the public good. At least where the individual can avoid for himself the moral complications of borrowed money, he should be careful to do so. And we all know how difficult it is in any case to keep covetous desires under strict control in our handling of our money affairs. Money is certainly *a* root of many evils.

43

Control of Sex

THIS chapter can be short and clear: for it deals not at all with sex as such but with the control of sex. That control is partly a control of the body, and in particular of what are nowadays so often referred to as 'the genitals'. In a less scientific and more personal period they were called the private parts, and that they essentially are. Of course boys and girls as they grow up must be told what they are for; and though in my youth we were able to sort that out mostly for ourselves, that is far less possible today. The essential thing is that they are our own private possessions, the use and control of which rests entirely with us.

But, as every growing boy or girl discovers, there is a direct channel of communication between the private parts (physical) and the mental images which suggest themselves and evoke pleasurable and exciting images (spiritual), and both are very difficult to control. No adolescent is altogether happy to masturbate: he feels it to be a loss of control (how serious he does not know) of himself, of his thoughts and of his acts; it gives him some sense of failure and generally some feeling of shame too. At the same time for a boy it brings a real release from a physical tension which mental images have made almost uncontrollable. That is his personal problem of self-control. The essential thing is that the sense of personal responsibility is not eroded, that the private parts and the private thoughts remain private and their control a real test of a man or woman's worth.

A boy is fortunate if his heterosexual impulses are not active in his earlier years. He is unwise if when he becomes conscious of them he lets them lead him into any but the most trivial and casual expression of them. If and when he comes to find himself in danger of an approach to fornication (nowadays referred to as sexual intercourse or even in a ghastly misuse of words 'making love'), the plain human truth is that the private parts of his personality are his alone and the private parts of her personality are hers alone and that he has no conceivable right to invade her privacy nor to excite his own, to take such a liberty, and that under conditions in which he cannot shoulder responsibility for his action in terms of spiritual consequences to the two moral beings concerned. The existence of contraceptives is only accidentally relevant. They may not and often do not remove the danger of an unprovided for baby: but in any case, their existence may only mean that the readiness to surrender spiritual self-control and moral integrity has been made in advance of the passionate excuse.

A clear rule, the existence of which is to be recognised and respected by all Christians, helps everybody. The clear rule is no fornication, no adultery. For disobedience to it everyone must argue his or her case out with God.

The trouble is that books, journals, pictures proceeding from editors, some at least of whom would never want to be thought of as guilty of promoting promiscuity or pornography, deliberately exploit temptations to think of and desire the physical pleasures of fornication. Editors are responsible not only for the control of their own sex impulses in their own lives but also for the help or hindrance they have given to those into whose hands their publications come. Nobody doubts that some control is necessary. Nobody thinks that each can be left to follow his own sex impulses and desires uncontrolled. Each of us, wittingly or unwittingly, helps others to perceive their own burdens of restraint and responsibility. A more serious thing is that many scientific professors of sex knowledge and of sociology assure the public that the rule of 'no fornication, no adultery' is unscientific and that their studies of the subject show that it is unnatural and therefore unnecessary to respect it. Thus they combine with the existence of contraceptives to remove restraints and to persuade adolescents and adults alike to accept their (unscientific) easement of the moral code. Anyone can defy or deny a code. That is a purely destructive act. Those who are so ready to destroy codes of sex restraint do not put anything socially constructive in their place: and do nothing to engage the interest and obedience of those who are seeking to maintain a sound morality of sex control. And all the endless talk about sex is increasingly profitless and *ad nauseam*.

I have seen one relevant suggestion, which might prove to be worth serious consideration. There are some young people today for whom for many good reasons marriage is not an immediate possibility and the responsibilities of home making not yet tolerable. They should not be led to think of fornication as a way out. How can they be helped? If a young man and a young woman become responsibly involved and develop a settled desire to incur full personal responsibility for one another, and if they come to feel that to anticipate marriage is not necessarily blameworthy but is called for as part of their committal of themselves to one another, there might be a good deal to be said for the revival of betrothal as a real and significant social and religious custom with a practical meaning.

It would have to take place with the full consent of the two families concerned. It would be a family event. It would in fact be a sacramental act made as indeed marriage itself is, essentially by the two persons, the two parties to the betrothal, themselves. After that sexual intercourse between them would not be regarded as in the moral sense fornication. Such an ecclesiastical up-grading of betrothal could not be made by one Church alone. If made and endorsed by agreement between the Churches of this country (with or without the consent of the Church of Rome), it would be seen by the public to be not in any way a concession by the Churches to permissiveness, but on the contrary as creating a new Church ceremony to meet, by a way of pastoral care which does not betray any principle, the urgent human needs of particular people upon whom the conditions of modern life were pressing unfairly.

There is the problem of whether or not to remarry divorced persons in church. Of course any Church that wants to is free to do so: but thereby it confuses its witness to the Christian principle of lifelong marriage, and unless it accepts all who apply must have a court or courts to decide who shall be accepted and who not, a decision which can only rest on estimates of spiritual worthiness. It is more sensible for a Church to decline to marry any divorced persons in church and to show its pastoral care in admitting such as are seen to be in good faith to be communicants.

44

Attitude to Work

Dr. Schweitzer once said that work was a man's response to life. That is a good definition. Work is a response to a situation. There is no real distinction between times at work and times of leisure. Both are equally a response to a situation, a positive response to which a positive attention and interest is given. Children ask for something to do. Men who have retired from their employed service are often miserable because they cannot find anything to employ them to which they can give a personal attention and interest, and are reduced to pottering. We are sometimes told that in the future people will only have to 'work' for a few hours each day and will have 'leisure' or free time in abundance. What that would mean in fact is that for a few hours they would be paid to work at a set task and for the rest they would be free to choose their work to suit themselves. That would indeed be a nightmare world. If work is a man's response to life, then he must be giving the same quality of work from himself all the time, whether he is being paid for it by others or not. A man's or a woman's attitude to work must be all of a piece, an expression of personal efficiency, a tribute of personal worth. Each Christian has to work out his own salvation, and by so doing help others to work out theirs.

All work from an honest person must be honest work whether he is technically 'at work' or 'off work'. Many people will be able to express their personal efficiency best in the work they choose to do in their leisure time—in their garden, in painting, in music or reading or in any other honest and useful employment which includes of course physical exercise and social enjoyment in due proportions. They will find there the great truth that if any man's work is to be profitable to himself or to other people, he must love his work and the more skilful he gets at it the greater will be his love for it or rather his love in it. As we saw earlier, no love means anything to we men unless it is linked with a sense of responsibility and in this case with a sense of responsibility to and so for the work in hand, for our handiwork, which is part of our life's work. It is out of this sense of responsibility that we become according to our ability professionals and it is as we become in this sense professionals that we become truly amateurs—lovers of our work, lovers of life, and in it all lovers of our fellow men and of God in them.

But if we are to pay our own way in life we have to earn. And when we go to work, we have to be paid for it by a salary or by wages or by selling what our skill has produced in our own workshop. They are all different ways of earning. It is sometimes said that all 'working men' have to sell is their labour. That is of course not true of any but the lowest grades of labour and is not true even of them. They are not selling anything. They are offering as their contribution to some kind of co-operative effort their physical energies, their mental processes, their acquired skills, their capacity for honest work, themselves as free men. The old legend said that because of his first act of disobedience (to which his wife had tempted him) Adam was driven out of the garden, where he did not have to work for his living, into the harsh world where the ground itself brings forth thorns and thistles for him to cope with and where Adam had to win his bread and be

the breadwinner for his family in the sweat of his face till
he returns to the earth from which he came. 'For dust thou
art and to dust thou shalt return'. Not surprisingly the
next thing to happen is a murderous trade dispute—
between Cain who tilled the ground and Abel who kept
sheep. That is what happens if the attitude to work gets
distorted. Eve was not really the trouble maker and Adam
the weak one. It is the male who causes the troubles by
his inadequate desires. Work is not in itself a punishment,
but a social necessity and the salvation of a man's soul.
And all workers of every sort must work together in co-
operation and not against each other in cut-throat competition if a nation is to be at all healthy and wholesome.

Thus by reaction against the old legend we are put to
the right way and to the right attitude to work and to all
work. In this economic world, it is necessary that money
values shall be assigned to different kinds of work, and
that work should be paid for by the time spent and the
thing done. For that purpose work must be *measured*, and
measured by objective standards and paid by 'yardsticks'
and paid in 'solid' cash. And all that would be surpassingly
hard among strictly honest men: it becomes a dreadful
mixture of deep tragedy and high comedy among the
'men of the world', working not for the sake of the job but
for what singly or by joint effort they can get out of the
national economy for themselves.

Christian and citizen can do no more than their best
to work honestly and to good ends in all things, to earn
honestly and to spend honestly, and to find their deepest
satisfaction not in the money received or spent but in the
reward that we all get from any job of work well done.

45

Drudgery and Distractions

ALL work entails drudgery—dull, monotonous or mean work. Some of it can be put onto machines or computers and so be done faster and better: but much of it cannot. A great deal of real life is dull, monotonous and meaningless and inevitably a great deal of the work which men and women have to do will be some kind of drudgery. The sensible man will school himself to like it, nor is that really difficult. There is a positive enjoyment to be got out of taking the drudgery in one's stride as part of the job of life to be done cheerfully and therefore well and with a good will. The grumbler will encourage himself to resent the drudgery, will do it indifferently and will make life unpleasant for himself and for his fellow workers and probably for his family too. He will breed discontent and be a ready prey for the demagogue and the disaffected. The masterful man will find slaves to do the drudgery at his bidding.[1] In any group—community, Church, college or other combine—it is devoutly to be hoped for the good of all that the sensible people will be able to set the tone so that the doing of the drudgery well is redeemed from dullness by the sense of working together at what must be done.

There will always be some who welcome any distraction which will relieve them from the drudgery of the daily

[1] Like most words, 'masterful' has at least two different meanings. The truly masterful man will be in whatever company as one that serveth and all will be his friends and slaves. The wrongly masterful man will be as one that wants to be master in his company and will have slaves but few friends.

round and the common task. We are all prone to welcome a distraction just because it takes our minds off what we are doing and all the more if it can present itself to our minds as something interesting or valuable or worthwhile in itself. At once the business of assessing priorities comes into view; and if the distraction seems to be worth more in itself than the appointed drudgery, we can quickly persuade ourselves where duty lies. There is danger in the present day idea that the younger generation must of right and indeed of duty pursue the adventurous, the daring, the ideal to the neglect of the more humdrum drudgery of the work in hand. It is not merely that the individual damages his own integrity and possibilities of service to the community by avoiding what only doing the drudgery can teach him. It is also that not all are able to scale the adventurous and the ideal heights with profit to themselves or others. They may find it more difficult to climb down again than it was to ascend on the wings of aspiration or corporate enthusiasm. It is of course right and necessary for the younger generation, for students, for the adventurous to explore ideas of every kind according to their interests and abilities: but these are ideas only and no one should be so impetuous as to tie himself to a speculative idea, to worship it as an ideal, and to forsake other ideals for this one service. That is only a form of idolatry. Here is the root trouble of all the unrest among idealists and idolaters which is travelling round the world today as a kind of universal disease. It is due, like every other moving tide in human affairs and in people of all generations, to a great mixture of motives, ranging from relatively pure idealism to the various kinds of adulterated idealism and lust for power or exhibitionism. In the past exponents of the Christian religion have often tended to preach its blessings as a remedy to distract people from the miseries of the present. It is a modern technique for idealists to stoke up all the grievances and distresses and injustices which abound in the world so that people will concentrate on what is beyond immediate remedy and continue to tolerate evils which are close at hand, in either case judging by material standards of what can be seen and heard. Ideals are very delicate plants and need careful spiritual discrimination. Unfortunately some of the activists who are also idealists get no further than the conviction that they must destroy what is, the existing order, as being *ex hypothesis* bad beyond redemption, when they have not yet got any clear or workable idea of what to put in its place.

The moral of all this is that we must not allow ourselves to be distracted by any diverting ideas away from the doing of the job in hand, drudgery and all. The job in hand of any student—and we all remain students all our lives—is to study and in studying to get not merely a skill but also a wisdom, an understanding of the methods of reasonable thinking and an understanding of the ways of men past and present. The job in hand of the trade union leader is to study how industry may be conducted to the combined advantage of employers and employed and of the country as a whole, and then as a leader himself to promote wise behaviour. The job in hand of the employer of capital is precisely the same. And so on to all professions, refusing all the solicitations to distract from the job in hand to some private or party or partisan kind of work, or to distract to unlovely forms of self-indulgence to luxurious living or hardening of the spiritual arteries.

The Christian and the citizen alike will try to keep to his job and not to be distracted ever from it—the job to be a useful, reasonable, profitable and generous servant of the community.

And here it is to be noted that the lowly man who goes on daily adding his 'one to one' may achieve more in terms of the spiritual values than a more ambitious man 'aiming at a million'. It is in the course of doing simple things gracefully and with a care for others that the kingdom of God comes among men. It was a very weatherbeaten preacher in the Old Testament who said: 'whatever your hand finds to do, do it with your might'. It is good advice, even though the reason he gives is not—'for there is no work, or thought or knowledge or wisdom in Hades, to which you are going'. Jesus Christ gave a better incentive. He knew the value of good workmanship in little things, and the reward of hearing from the master in charge 'Well done, good and faithful servant'.

46

A Parting Word

My last word to Christian and citizen alike begins with a quotation:

> Salt is good; but if the salt has lost its saltness, how shall it be restored? Have salt in yourselves, and be at peace with one another.

I suggest that the salt of life is not love but a sense of personal responsibility to oneself, to one's neighbours, to God, to life, enriched by fellowship with the Holy Spirit, the Lord, the Giver of Life.

Too much salt makes life unpalatable. Too little salt makes life tasteless. The due seasoning is to be found in an appropriate sense of responsibility which is expressed in the activities of a truly balanced love. Each person must discover for himself what load of responsibility he can reasonably try to carry on his own shoulders as his contribution to his own load-carrying and to the load-carrying of his community. To carry too small a load must be due to his own lack of imagination, his own lack of ability or to sheer selfishness. To try to carry a load too heavy for his own strength may be grand, heroic, a true evidence of the readiness of his desire to serve: it may possibly be foolish, out of due proportion, involving an over-estimate of one's own abilities or importance: it may be ill-advised; even so it may by the grace of God be made fruitful in good work by God's enabling. Who can tell? No one can tell except by walking by faith and learning from experience.

It is only by people having salt in themselves, this kind of salt, that a true peace becomes possible among men of good will. Only salt saves peace from being mere passive surrender or mere acceptance of failure. Salt preserves peace and gives, even in defeat, a creative savour and a promise of redemption.

How shall the tast of salt, its saltness, be preserved (or restored) in the lives of citizens and of Christians? That question I can only answer by another quotation which gives a purpose, a promise, and a sure and certain hope to the everyday life of everyone:

> Seek first the kingdom of God and his righteousness, and all these things shall be yours as well.

All these things? Jesus Christ had just mentioned some of our wants—food, drink, clothing, and went on to say that secular men and nations seek all these necessities and that God, our Father in heaven, knows how necessary they are to us. But salt? It comes from a sense of responsibility to the kingdom of God and from an active service of it here in the kingdoms of this world. And of course each person has to form his own idea of God and of the kingdom and of his service to it. Salt and its true savour comes from loyalty to Christ himself and service to him, in the power of the Holy Spirit.

And so from this latest chapter we always must go back again to the first chapters and learn afresh with daily increasing confidence. And all the time *joyfully on to the kingdom of God and to Christ our Saviour and King* with a more abounding thankfulness and a more profound possession of the Peace of God.